《笃行中文》4

DUXING CHINESE

笃行中文

毛通文 黄建军/主编

厦门大学出版社 XIAMEN UNIVERSITY PRESS
国家一级出版社
全国百佳图书出版单位

图书在版编目(CIP)数据

笃行中文.4/毛通文,黄建军主编.—厦门:厦门大学出版社,2021.12
ISBN 978-7-5615-8435-4

Ⅰ.①笃… Ⅱ.①毛… ②黄… Ⅲ.①汉语—对外汉语教学—教材 Ⅳ.①H195.4

中国版本图书馆 CIP 数据核字(2021)第 262571 号

出 版 人 郑文礼
责任编辑 刘 璐
封面设计 蔡炜荣
技术编辑 朱 楷

出版发行 厦门大学出版社
社　　址 厦门市软件园二期望海路 39 号
邮政编码 361008
总　　机 0592-2181111 0592-2181406(传真)
营销中心 0592-2184458 0592-2181365
网　　址 http://www.xmupress.com
邮　　箱 xmup@xmupress.com
印　　刷 厦门集大印刷有限公司

开本 787 mm×1 092 mm 1/16
印张 8.75
插页 1
字数 158 千字
版次 2021 年 12 月第 1 版
印次 2021 年 12 月第 1 次印刷
定价 45.00 元

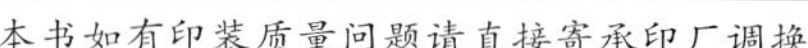

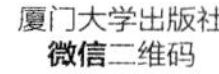
厦门大学出版社
微信二维码

厦门大学出版社
微博二维码

编写说明

《笃行中文》（1～4）由厦门大学汉语国际推广南方基地与泰国皇太后大学孔子学院联合编写。本套教材的主要教学对象是国外大学非汉语专业本科生及中学生。教材以中国教育部中外语言交流合作中心《新汉语水平考试HSK大纲（一～六级）》为依据，贯彻“考教结合”“以考促教”“以考促学”的理念，注重培养学生学习汉语的兴趣和中文实际应用能力。教材每册包含约300个汉语词汇和相应的语法知识，带“*”的生词为超纲词；按课堂教学45课时、课后练习45课时设计。学生学完第一册可达到HSK二级水平，学完第二册可达HSK三级水平，学完第三、四册可达HSK四级水平。

为了方便学生课后练习中文，我们专门设计了适合学生使用的网上练习与测试系统，学生可以方便地在电脑和手机上完成课后练习及测试，并可模拟HSK。

本套教材汲取了厦门大学各共建孔子学院多年的教学经验，以培养学生的听力和阅读能力为重点，兼顾汉字知识和与课文相关的中国文化知识。限于编者学识，疏漏谬误在所难免，恳请识者不吝赐教！

本教材在编写过程中得到厦门大学国际中文教育学院夏国香、刘玉川、彭涛老师的大力支持，泰国皇太后大学孔子学院于群老师对本套教材做了系统的审校；在编写各课“走近中国”栏目时，参考了百度百科中的“十二生肖”“二十四节气”“科举制”“文房四宝”“指南针”等条目，并做了改写；“汉字”栏目参考了《体验汉字（入门篇）》和《新实用汉语课本（第一册）》等教材，也做了相应改写，特此致谢！

《笃行中文》编写组

2020年12月10日

词类简称表
ABBREVIATIONS

noun	*n.*	名词 míngcí
verb	*v.*	动词 dòngcí
adjective	*adj.*	形容词 xíngróngcí
numeral	*num.*	数词 shùcí
measure word	*m.*	量词 liàngcí
pronoun	*pron.*	代词 dàicí
adverb	*adv.*	副词 fùcí
preposition	*prep.*	介词 jiècí
conjunction	*conj.*	连词 liáncí
particle	*part.*	助词 zhùcí
interjection	*int.*	叹词 tàncí
auxiliary verb	*aux.*	能愿动词 néngyuàn dòngcí

目 录

CONTENTS

第一课 你把行李拿下来吧

学习目标 Learning Objectives

1. 掌握乘坐飞机和租房的相关词汇

Understand the vocabulary related to taking airplanes and renting houses

2. 运用"主语＋把＋宾语＋动词＋趋向补语"强调动作对象的位移

Use "S+*Ba*+O+Verb+Direction Complement" to emphasize the locational change of a certain object by an action

课文 1 Text 1

送欧文去机场

安娜：喂，欧文，我快到你楼下了，你把行李拿下来吧。

欧文：我已经下楼了，正在把行李推出去。

安娜：好的，你等我把车开过去。

欧文：我看到你的车了。好，车就停这儿吧。我先把行李搬到车上。

安娜：快上车吧！把安全带系好。

欧文：好。辛苦你了！

安娜：不客气。祝贺你通过美国大使馆的面试！

欧文：谢谢，我收到面试通过的消息时特别激动！不过我还得实习一个月，实习结束了才是正式的翻译。

安娜：你实习肯定没问题的！你的航班是几点的？

欧文：是八点的，大约十点半到北京。

安娜：那我得把车开快点。已经六点了，到机场还得半个小时呢。

欧文：好的，要是六点半能到机场，就来得及。

安娜：没问题。

词汇 1 Vocabulary 1

1	推	tuī	*v.*	to push
2	系	jì	*v.*	to tie; to fasten (HSK5 Word)
3	祝贺	zhùhè	*v.*	to congratulate
4	通过	tōngguò	*v.*	to pass
			prep.	through
5	面试 *	miànshì	*n.*	interview
			v.	to interview
6	消息	xiāoxi	*n.*	information; news
7	激动	jīdòng	*adj.*	excited; emotional
8	得	děi	*aux.*	ought to; need to
9	正式	zhèngshì	*adj.*	formal

课文 2 Text 2

在机场

安娜：到了。我先把车停好，再帮你把行李推进去。

欧文：不着急，我刚收到消息，航班推迟到九点起飞了。

安娜：现在才六点半，要不你先进机场休息休息？

欧文：好的，我得先把护照拿出来。

安娜：对，你可以用护照把登机牌提前打印出来。

欧文：呀！我的护照呢？
安娜：你不会把护照忘在家里了吧？
欧文：我太粗心了！你快送我回去取护照吧！
安娜：好，你下次收拾行李千万得认真一点。今天要不是航班推迟了，就来不及了。
欧文：知道了。下次坐飞机我一定提前检查护照。

词汇 2 Vocabulary 2

1	推迟	tuīchí	*v.*	to postpone; to delay 推：to push　迟：late
2	要不	yàobù	*conj.*	or else; how about... (HSK5 Word)
3	登机牌	dēngjī pái		boarding pass 登机：to board　牌：card
4	提前	tíqián	*v.*	to shift to an earlier time
5	打印	dǎyìn	*v.*	to print
6	呀	yā	*int.*	used alone to express surprise
7	粗心	cūxīn	*adj.*	careless; thoughtless
8	取	qǔ	*v.*	to get; to fetch
9	要不是 *	yàobúshì	*conj.*	if it were not for

课文 3 Text 3

在北京租房

我和安娜在上海读了三年汉语专业，今年夏天我们终于硕士毕业了。她留在上海继续读博士，我来到北京一个大使馆工作。

上周五早上六点半，安娜就开车把我送到上海机场了。可是我太马虎了，没提前检查护照，到机场才发现把护照忘在家里了。幸亏航班推迟了，安娜送我回家取了护照，我才赶上了飞机。

我坐了两个半小时飞机来到了北京。在北京租房的时候，我遇到了特别好的房东。看房的那天，房东让我留下来吃饭，我们聊了聊。房东姓王，是北京大学的教授，房东的妻子姓张，是一名护士。王教授很成功，不仅会说三种语言，翻译研究还做得特别好。他们的儿子在国外留学，所以把一个房间空出来了。我把这个房间租下来了，打算跟王教授做做语言翻译方面的研究。

我今天把房间的照片给安娜发过去了。她看了照片，说我的房间还有点空，可以再买点家具让生活更方便。她说会在上海等我的好消息，要是有空会来北京看我。

词汇 3 Vocabulary 3

1	留	liú	*v.*	to stay; to remain
2	马虎	mǎhu	*adj.*	careless; negligent
3	幸亏	xìngkuī	*adv.*	fortunately; luckily (HSK5 Word)
4	房东	fángdōng	*n.*	landlord
5	教授	jiàoshòu	*n.*	professor
6	护士	hùshi	*n.*	nurse
7	语言	yǔyán	*n.*	language
8	研究	yánjiū	*n.*	research
			v.	to research
9	空	kòng	*v.*	to empty
		kòng	*n.*	free time; space
		kōng	*adj.*	vacant; unoccupied; empty

语 法 Grammar

"把"字句 + 趋向补语（S + *Ba* + O + Verb + Direction Complement）

"'把'字句 + 趋向补语"在汉语中用来表达动作使确定的人或者事物发生了位置上的改变。例如：

A direction complement is a complement used to describe the direction of a verb. The *Ba*-sentence with a directional complement is used to express the locational change of an action towards a certain person or thing. For example,

1. 安娜请欧文把行李拿下来。
2. 欧文想先把护照拿出来。
3. 安娜开车把欧文送回去取护照。

走近中国 A Touch of China

房与家
——中国人的房子情结

在中国的文化语境中，当人们提到"家"这个字的时候，总会激起对某个地点、某个人群的联想，以及一些正面的感觉，如安全感、温暖感、归属感等。社会单位的"家"和居住空间的"房屋"之间有着密切的关系。在地方文化中，只有人们修建了堂屋，一个家才获得社会的承认，一个家庭的成立也必须立足于具体的房屋上。今天的人们总是将房子作为婚姻的一个前提，其背后的文化机制也许正在于此。

中国人历来有房子情结，自古就把房子当成安身立命之所。在中国的历史文化中，没有住宅就意味着没有"家"，意味着生活的不稳定。"居无定所""流离失所""寄人篱下"说的都是极为落魄和穷困的人。从文化根源上分析，热衷于买房子与中国的传统文化有很大关系。一方面，中华文化的根主要在农耕文化，农耕文化反映在个体身上，则是追求安定、规避风险。中国人渴求农耕时期身体和灵魂共同附着在土地上的那种稳定感，即使离开农村进入城市后仍然保持着这种心理惯性。因此，拥有稳定的工作和自己的房子在中国是刚性需求。另一方面，与农耕文化相映衬的是儒家文化，儒家文化推崇"家族传承"和"家族至上"。在这种"家族传承"的文化基因下，中国人买房，不仅仅关乎个体，而是一个家庭乃至两个家庭的大事；不仅关乎家庭、家族的面子问题，而且也关乎娶妻生子、繁衍后代的终身大事。

在现代社会，"安居乐业"作为一种生活理想，洋溢着浓浓的亲情，然而过犹不及。现在的中国年轻人面对高房价的压力，当自己的经济水平实现不了"买房置业"时，不妨先行租房，只要用心经营、用爱经营，"此心安处是吾乡"。

House and Home

—Chinese People's Complex in Houses

In the Chinese cultural context, when people mention the word "home", they always associate it with a certain place and a certain group of people, as well as positive feelings like a sense of security, warmth, and belonging, etc. There is a close relationship between the "home" of the social unit and the "house" of the residential space. In the local culture, only when people build a hall can a family be recognized by the society, and the establishment of a family must also be based on a specific house. People today always regard the house as a prerequisite for marriage, and the cultural mechanism behind it may be here.

Chinese have always had a house complex, and since ancient times they have regarded the house as a place to settle down. In Chinese history and culture, the absence of a house means that there is no "home", which means the instability of life. "Without a permanent house" and "being under somebody's roof" are all extremely destitute and impoverished people. From the perspective of cultural roots, the pursuit for a house has a lot to do with traditional Chinese culture. On the one hand, the root of Chinese culture lies mainly in farming culture. Farming culture is reflected in individuals, which is to pursue stability and avoid risks. Chinese people are eager for the sense of stability that the body and soul attach to the land together during the farming period. Even after leaving the countryside and entering the city, they still maintain this psychological inertia.

Therefore, having a stable job and owning a house are rigid demands in China. On the other hand, consistent with the farming culture, Confucianism promotes "family inheritance" and "family supremacy". Under this "family inheritance" cultural gene, buying a house is not only about the individual, but a major event for one or even two families; it is not only about the family and the face of the family, but also about crucial life events like getting married, having children, and reproducing offspring.

In modern times, "living and working in peace and contentment" is an ideal of life, permeated with family love, but going beyond the limit is as bad as falling short. Nowadays, young people are faced with the pressure of high housing prices. When their economic level cannot achieve "buying a house or a property", they may wish to rent a house first. As long as they manage with heart and love, "home is where the heart belongs".

注释 Notes

Cǐ xīn ān chù shì wú xiāng.
此 心 安 处 是 吾 乡 。

Home is where the heart belongs.

诗人白居易曾写过"我生本无乡，心安是归处"。受到此诗的启发，宋代词人苏轼写下了一句词："试问岭南应不好，却道：此心安处是吾乡"，表达了旷达乐观的人生哲学。

The poet Bai Juyi once wrote, "I have no hometown in my life, and a peace of mind is my home". Inspired by this, the Song Dynasty poet Su Shi wrote, "People say life in Lingnan is not good, but the truth is that home is where the heart belongs", which expressed a broad-minded and optimistic philosophy of life.

学而时习之 Practice Makes Progress

(一) 选词填空 (Choose the correct words for the blanks)

A. 通过　　B. 登机牌　　C. 粗心　　D. 房东

1. 在机场，用护照可以提前打印(　　)。
2. 欧文很(　　)，他把护照忘在家里了！

3. 欧文的（　　）是一位北京大学的教授。

4. 欧文（　　）大使馆的面试了，特别开心。

（二）连词成句（Form sentences with the words given）

1. 我　推进去　帮你　行李　把

____

2. 得　他　一个月　还　实习

____

3. 下次　护照　检查　一定　提前　我

____

4. 发过去　照片　把　我　给她　了

____

（三）阅读理解（Read and choose the right option）

欧文通过了大使馆的面试，要去北京工作了。安娜把欧文送到了机场，欧文才发现把护照忘在家里了。安娜又开车把欧文送回家取了护照。幸亏航班推迟了，要不然欧文一定来不及了。

1. 根据上文，欧文发现护照在哪里？（　　）

A. 车里　B. 家里　C. 机场　D. 学校

2. 幸亏航班怎么了，要不然欧文就来不及了？（　　）

A. 起飞了　B. 降落了　C. 出发了　D. 推迟了

（四）口语练习（Speaking task）

请用下面的词，向你的小组介绍一次自己的旅行经历，并选择两个句子写下来。

A. 提前　B. 激动

C. 粗心　D. 得

1. ____________________

2. ____________________

（五）看图写句子（Look at the pictures and make sentences with the words given）

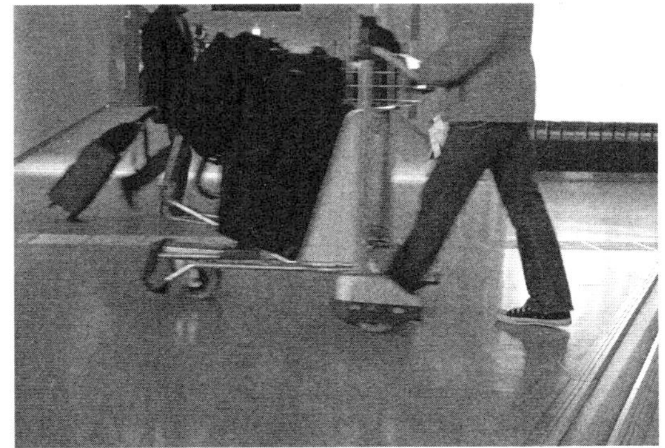

推

____

祝贺

____

激动

____

推迟

____

第二课　同事表扬我做得好

学习目标 Learning Objectives

1. 掌握入职新工作的相关词汇

Understand the vocabulary related to starting new jobs

2. 运用兼语句表示指令或因果关系

Use pivotal sentences to give orders or denote cause-effect relations

Text 1

在北京的出租车上

欧文：师傅，您好，去美国大使馆。

司机：你好！请系好安全带，大约二十分钟到。

欧文：好的。今天是我工作的第一天，好紧张啊！

司机：小伙子，你是要去大使馆工作吗？

欧文：对，美国大使馆让我去当翻译。

司机：不用紧张。你的普通话说得很好！学了多久了？

欧文：从我中学开始，妈妈就请了老师教我学汉语。而且我还有好多中国同学帮我练习普通话。

司机：你是哪个国家的？我从来没听过哪个外国人的汉语说得这么流利！

欧文：我是美国人，普通话还不像中国人说得那么好。

司机：你当翻译肯定没问题。翻译这个工作好，可以认识很多新朋友，还对中美两国之间的友谊有帮助。加油！

欧文：好的，我一定好好努力，让两国关系变得更友好！

司机：美国大使馆到了。

欧文：辛苦您了，麻烦帮我打张发票。

司机：好的，这是发票，你拿好。祝你一切顺利！

欧文：谢谢师傅！

词汇 1　Vocabulary 1

1	师傅	shīfu	*n.*	master; an honorific address for older men; informal way to address drivers
2	紧张	jǐnzhāng	*adj.*	nervous
3	小伙子	xiǎohuǒzi	*n.*	young man
4	普通话	pǔtōnghuà	*n.*	Mandarin (common speech of the Chinese language)
5	流利	liúlì	*adj.*	fluent
6	之	zhī	*part.*	possessive particle (literary equivalent of 的)
7	友谊	yǒuyì	*n.*	friendship
8	友好	yǒuhǎo	*adj.*	friendly 友：friend　好：good
9	发票	fāpiào	*n.*	invoice (HSK5 Word)

课文 2　Text 2

在美国大使馆

同事：欧文，欢迎你来到北京，祝贺你成为美国大使馆的一名翻译。我们有一个见面礼要送给你。

欧文：太感谢了！这是中国茶叶吗？

同事：是的，这种茶喝起来有点苦，不知道你会不会喜欢？

欧文：喜欢！茶叶苦一点没关系，对身体好。我正好带了些甜的上海小吃，请大家一起尝尝。

同事：谢谢！这是你的合同，实习期工资是正式翻译的百分之八十。

欧文：好的，实习期我需要做什么？

同事：在实习期，我们会安排一个有经验的同事带你熟悉工作，主要是一些复印和传真工作需要你做。

欧文：好的，没问题。谢谢您！

同事：不客气，我带你去认识一下李想。

词汇 2 Vocabulary 2

1	成为	chéngwéi	*v.*	to become
2	感谢	gǎnxiè	*v.*	to thank; to be grateful
3	苦	kǔ	*adj.*	bitter
4	合同	hétong	*n.*	contract (HSK5 Word)
5	工资	gōngzī	*n.*	wage; salary
6	百分之	bǎi fēn zhī		percent
7	经验	jīngyàn	*n.*	experience
8	复印	fùyìn	*v.*	to duplicate; to photocopy
9	传真	chuánzhēn	*v.*	to fax

课文 3 Text 3

开始北京的工作

差不多一个月前，我来到了美国大使馆，见到了热情友好的同事们。他们给我准备了中国茶叶做见面礼，使我很感动。大使馆给我安排了一个有经验的同事帮助我熟悉工作，她叫李想。

我有一个月的实习期来适应北京的工作。这一个月还是比较轻松的，李想主要让我负责一些材料与发票的复印与传真工作。李想觉得我做事很认真，表扬我做得好。

通过实习，我积累了很多工作经验。还有几天，实习期就要结束了，我就要拿到合同，成为美国大使馆的正式翻译了。尽管同事们说之后会比较辛苦，但我已经做好了吃苦的准备。

安娜担心我一个人在北京不习惯，鼓励我好好适应这里的生活。她说我的工作会让中美两国之间的关系变得更加友好。我也这样觉得。我一定会为两国的友谊而努力工作！

词汇 3　Vocabulary 3

1	使	shǐ	*v.*	to cause; to make
2	感动	gǎndòng	*v.*	to make someone feel touched
			adj.	touched
3	负责	fùzé	*v.*	to be in charge of
4	材料	cáiliào	*n.*	material
5	与	yǔ	*conj.*	and (literary equivalent of 和)
6	表扬	biǎoyáng	*v.*	to praise
7	积累	jīlěi	*v.*	to accumulate
8	鼓励	gǔlì	*v.*	to encourage
			n.	encouragement
9	而	ér	*conj.*	indicating causal relation or contrast

语　法　Grammar

兼语句（Pivotal Sentences）

兼语句是现代汉语中的一种特殊句式，指由兼语短语充当谓语或独立成句的句子。兼语短语由两个动词短语组成，前一个动词的宾语是第二个动词的主语。例如：

In Chinese, there is a special sentence structure called pivotal sentence, which consists of a pivotal phrase to form a sentence or to predicate. A pivotal phrase is usually made up of two verbs and an element that can be treated as the object of the first verb but the subject of the second one. For example,

1. 同事们祝贺欧文成为一名翻译。
2. 欧文请司机打了一张发票。
3. 李想让欧文负责复印工作。

A Touch of China

中华传统礼仪

中国素有“礼仪之邦”之称，有懂礼、习礼、守礼、重礼的文化传统，“礼”是中华传统文化的核心，是形式与内容的完美统一。著名史学家钱穆说过，礼是整个中国人世界里一切习俗行为的准则。要了解中国文化，就要了解中国传统礼仪。

法国启蒙思想家孟德斯鸠以西方人的眼光看中国人的“礼”，认为中国人的生活完全以“礼”为指南。这里的“礼”有礼义与礼仪两层含义。礼义指礼的精神和原则；礼仪指礼的仪节，是礼的具体表现形式。可以说礼义是不变的，礼仪却是可变的。

从礼义角度而言，礼仪文化的核心在于仁，在于爱他人，这不仅是一种关心、友爱的态度，更是思想层面的尊重，即不把自己的想法和意志强加给他人。礼仪文化的本质在于敬，即在待人接物方面表现出的尊重与恭敬的态度。在与人交往时要放低姿态，谦恭待人、尊重他人，以赢得他人的尊重。礼仪文化的根本在于和。“和合”理念是中华民族一贯的文化追求，追求和谐是中国传统、民族心理和社会生活的重要特征，包括个体身心的和谐、群己关系的和谐和家国的和谐三个方面。

从礼仪形式而言，在中国古代社会，上至国家典章制度，下至百姓衣食住行及行为方式，无不贯穿着“礼”的精神，并形成了一系列繁复的礼仪规程。在现代中国人的日常生活中，传统礼仪已经大大简化，但“礼”依然无时不在、无处不在。例如，各种正式场合的座位讲究按社会地位的高低和辈分排列；晚辈不得直呼长辈的姓名；节庆期间，晚辈要向尊长致敬；宴席上客人需待主人举杯劝饮或执筷劝食后方可动筷；在汉语表达方面，注重敬语和谦词的使用，等等。

Traditional Chinese Etiquette

China is known as the “state of etiquette” and it has a cultural tradition of understanding etiquette, ritual practice, observing and emphasizing etiquette. “Rites” are the core of traditional Chinese culture and are the perfect unity of form and content. The famous historian Qian Mu said, “Ritual is the norm for all customs and behaviors in the entire Chinese world”. To understand Chinese culture, one must understand traditional Chinese etiquette.

Montesquieu, a French enlightenment thinker, viewed Chinese “rites” from the perspective of westerners, and believed that Chinese people’s lives were guided by “rites”. The word “rites” here has two meanings: ritual philosophy and etiquette. The meaning of ritual philosophy refers to the spirit and principles of etiquette; etiquette refers to the specific manifestation. It can be said that ritual philosophy is unchanged, but etiquette is variable.

From the perspective of ritual philosophy, the core of etiquette culture lies in benevolence and love for others. This is not only a caring and friendly attitude, but also an ideological respect, that is not imposing one’s own ideas and will on others. The essence of etiquette culture lies in respect, that is the attitude of respect and respect shown in dealing with people and things. When interacting with others, one should lower his stance, be courteous and respect others, in order to win the respect of others. The essence of etiquette culture lies in harmony. The concept of “harmony and unity” is the consistent cultural pursuit of the Chinese nation. The pursuit of harmony is an important feature of Chinese tradition, national psychology, and social life. It includes three aspects: the harmony of the individual’s body and mind, the harmony between the group and the self, and the harmony between the family and the country.

In terms of etiquette, in ancient Chinese society, from the national ordinance system to the people's clothing, food, housing, transportation and behavior, the spirit of "rituals" has been run through, and a series of complicated etiquette rules has been formed. In the daily lives of modern Chinese people, traditional etiquette has been greatly simplified, but ritual is still everywhere at all times. For example, seats in various formal occasions are arranged according to social status and generation; younger generations are not allowed to call their elders by their names directly; during festivals, younger generations must visit and respect the elders; guests at banquets need to wait for the host to raise a glass or hold chopsticks to persuade food first; in terms of Chinese expressions, honorific expressions are frequently used.

注 释 Notes

Héhé
和合

Harmony and Unity

"和合"，出自《墨子》，指和睦同心。它影响着中国人的宇宙观、天下观、家庭观和处世观等，在一定程度上规范了当代中国人的思维方式，也使中国成为世界和平发展的重要力量。

"和合", from the book *Mozi*, refers to harmony and unity, which affects the Chinese people's views on the universe, the world, the family and daily affairs. It regulates the way of thinking of contemporary Chinese people to some degree and also makes China an important force for the peaceful development of the world.

学而时习之 Practice Makes Progress

（一）选词填空（Choose the correct words for the blanks）

A. 流利　　B. 百分之　　C. 表扬　　D. 感动

1. 欧文实习的时候只能拿（　　）八十的工资。
2. 同事们都（　　）欧文工作做得好。

3. 同事们准备了见面礼，让欧文很（　　）。

4. 安娜的汉语说得越来越（　　）了。

（二）连词成句（Form sentences with the words given）

1. 普通话　很流利　的　说得　小伙子

____

2. 他　经验　了　实习期　积累

____

3. 她　负责　工作　打印　让我

____

4. 师傅　打　请　我　发票　了

____

（三）阅读理解（Read and choose the right option）

欧文开始了在美国大使馆的实习期工作。同事们给欧文准备了一个见面礼，是中国茶叶。大使馆还给欧文安排了一位有经验的同事，帮助欧文熟悉工作。欧文在实习期负责材料的复印和传真工作，积累了很多工作经验。

1. 根据上文，同事们给欧文准备了什么礼物？（　　）

A. 茶叶　　B. 咖啡　　C. 巧克力　　D. 蛋糕

2. 欧文实习期积累了什么？（　　）

A. 工作　　B. 经验　　C. 材料　　D. 帮助

（四）口语练习（Speaking task）

请用下面的词，向你的小组介绍一个同学，并选择两个句子写下来。

A. 友好　　B. 友谊
C. 感谢　　D. 感动

1. ____

2. ____

（五）看图写句子（Look at the pictures and make sentences with the words given）

感谢

____

工资

____

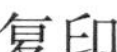

复印

____

材料

____

第三课　即使再难，我也不会放弃

学习目标 Learning Objectives

1. 掌握博士学习与生活相关词汇

Understand the vocabulary related to PhD students and their life

2. 运用“即使……，也……”表示结果不受假设影响

Use “即使……，也……” to express “even though..., ...still...”

课文 1 Text 1

在学校遇到张教授

安　娜：张教授，您好！您在这儿看报纸呀？

张教授：对，出太阳了，外面比较暖和。

安　娜：即使有太阳，现在外面温度也挺低的。您要注意，别感冒啦。

张教授：不会的。安娜，你读博士已经三个月了，感觉怎么样？

安　娜：我感觉读博士比读硕士难多了。

张教授：是的，尤其你是外国人，读汉语专业的博士会有很多困难。

安　娜：嗯，我知道。不过，我不想放弃。

张教授：对，你好不容易考上了博士，如果放弃就太可惜了。

安　娜：是的，即使再难，我也要继续读。我来中国就是为了学习和研究汉语。

张教授：你这种积极的态度特别好！

安　娜：谢谢您的鼓励！我去操场跑步了，下次上课再见。

张教授：好的，快去吧！

词汇 1 Vocabulary 1

1	即使	jíshǐ	*conj.*	even if; even though
2	温度	wēndu	*n.*	temperature
3	低	dī	*adj.*	low
			v.	to lower
4	困难	kùnnan	*adj.*	difficult; hard
			n.	difficulty; hardship
5	嗯	ǹg	*int.*	indicating approval, appreciation or agreement (HSK5 Word)
6	放弃	fàngqì	*v.*	to abandon; to give up
7	可惜	kěxī	*adj.*	regrettable; unfortunate
8	积极	jījí	*adj.*	active; positive
9	态度	tàidu	*n.*	attitude

课文 2 Text 2

在学校操场上

同学：安娜，你也来跑步呀？

安娜：是啊，这学期天气很凉快，我得多锻炼身体。等到下学期，在外面跑步就太冷了。

同学：我也不喜欢冬天跑步。你平时跑得快不快？

安娜：我跑得不快，100 米得 30 多秒吧。

同学：我也喜欢慢跑。有空的时候，我经常练习 5000 米慢跑。

安娜：你好厉害！我没耐心跑完 5000 米，我一般只跑 800 米。
同学：800 米也不错。即使只跑几百米，仍然对身体有好处。
安娜：嗯，我慢跑的目的主要是放松身心。
同学：想放松的话，我建议你跑步时听听流行音乐。
安娜：好主意，这样我自己跑步的时候就不无聊了！
同学：走，这次咱们一起跑吧。
安娜：好的！咱们边跑边聊。

词汇 2 Vocabulary 2

1	学期	xuéqī	*n.*	term; semester
2	凉快	liángkuai	*adj.*	cool
3	秒	miǎo	*m.*	second (unit of time)
4	耐心	nàixīn	*adj.*	patient
			n.	patience
5	仍然	réngrán	*adv.*	still; yet
6	目的	mùdì	*n.*	purpose; aim
7	流行	liúxíng	*adj.*	fashionable; popular
			v.	to become popular; (of a contagious disease, etc.) to spread
8	无聊	wúliáo	*adj.*	bored; boring
9	咱们	zánmen	*pron.*	we; us

课文 3 Text 3

在上海读博士

我在上海读博士差不多三个月了，我的老师是汉语专业的张教授。上学期博士面试结果出来的时候，同学们都很吃惊，他们不相信我竟然成了张教授的博士生。

虽然张教授对我很严格，但是我非常尊重他，我知道他严格是为了我好。由于我是外国人，张教授经常耐心地鼓励我。尤其是要用汉语写研究文章，对于我们外国人来说很困难。

在生活方面，我感觉上海的一切都很好。爸爸妈妈本来以为我一个人在中国生活会有困难，但是现在他们也相信我能够坚持下去，因为他们知道，研究汉语是我来中国的目的。

在学习方面，我压力很大，但是张教授的鼓励让我很有信心。我每天都严格要求自己，在图书馆看书看到很晚。即使用汉语写文章再难，我也不会放弃！

词汇 3 Vocabulary 3

1	结果	jiéguǒ	*n.*	result
			conj.	in the end
2	吃惊	chījīng	*v.*	to be shocked 吃：to eat 惊：surprise
3	严格	yángé	*adj.*	strict
			v.	to be strict with
4	尊重	zūnzhòng	*v.*	to respect
			adj.	respectful
			n.	respect
5	由于	yóuyú	*conj.*	because; since
6	文章	wénzhāng	*n.*	passage; article
7	对于	duìyú	*prep.*	with regards to
8	压力	yālì	*n.*	pressure; stress
9	信心	xìnxīn	*n.*	confidence

语　法　Grammar

即使……，也……（Even if/though..., ...still...）

“即使……，也……”表示结果或结论不受假设的情况影响。“即使”是连词，表示假设的让步，表示的条件可以是还没发生或实现的事情，也可以是与既成事实相反的事情。当有“还是”“仍然”等词时，“也”可以省略。例如：

“即使……，也……” means “even if/though..., ...still...”. The first clause (即使……) is a supposition or hypothesis, which is followed by an opposite statement or decision as the second clause. When words like “还是” and “仍然” appear to indicate “still”, “也” can be omitted. For example,

1. 即使有太阳，外面温度（也）还是很低的。
2. 即使只跑几百米，（也）仍然对身体有好处。
3. 即使写汉语文章再难，安娜也不会放弃。

走近中国　A Touch of China

只要功夫深，铁杵磨成针

“只要功夫深，铁杵磨成针”是中国的一句谚语，比喻只要有决心和毅力，再难的事情也能做成。

这句话出自中国古代的一个故事。传说唐朝著名诗人李白在小时候非常聪明但不爱学习，经常把书本丢下出去玩耍。有一天，李白碰到一个白发苍苍的老婆婆拿着一个铁棒在石头上磨，他觉得很好奇。李白问她在做什么，老婆婆说在磨绣花针。李白不相信，说这么粗的铁棒怎么可能磨成绣花针。老婆婆说只要天天磨，坚持下去，就可以磨成一根绣花针。李白深受感动，从此开始下决心用功读书，终于成为著名的大文豪。这个故事告诉后人，在遇到困难的时候，要勇于面对，并且肯下功夫，坚持就是胜利。

在中华文化经典中，还有很多与努力和毅力相关的故事，比如“水滴石穿”“愚公移山”等。“水滴石穿”是一个汉语成语，意思是水不断下滴，可以洞穿石头，比喻只要有恒心，不断努力，事情一定能成功。同样，“愚公移山”讲的也是“持之以恒，事必有成”的故事。《愚公移山》是战国时期思想家列子的一篇寓言，叙述了愚公和后辈面对堵住道路的两座大山，不畏艰难，坚持挖山，最终感动天帝将山挪走的故事。这个故事表现了中国古代劳动人民的毅力。

类似的汉语俗语还有“有志者事竟成”“世上无难事，只怕有心人”等，都说明了要克服困难就必须坚持不懈的道理，启发后人为了理想而长期奋斗。有的时候，即使不能完全达到预期结果，行动与坚持也一定会使事情有所进展，这与西方谚语“Perseverance Prevails”有异曲同工之妙。

Perseverance Prevails

“As long as you have perseverance, the iron rod can be ground into a needle” is a Chinese idiom, which indicates that as long as there is determination, difficult things can be easier too.

This sentence comes from an ancient Chinese story. According to legend, Li Bai, a famous poet in Tang Dynasty, was very smart when he was a child but he didn’t like learning. He often dropped his books to play. One day, Li Bai met a gray-haired old woman who was grinding an iron rod on a stone, and he was very curious. Li Bai asked her what she was doing, and the old woman said she was grinding embroidery needles. Li Bai didn’t believe it, saying how such a thick iron rod could be ground into embroidery needles. The old woman said that as long as she ground it every day and persisted, she could grind it into an embroidery needle. Li Bai was deeply moved, and from then on he determined to study hard and finally became a famous writer. The moral of this story is that when encountering difficulties, you must be brave enough to face them, and you must be willing to work hard. Perseverance makes victory.

In the Chinese cultural classics, there are many stories related to hard work and perseverance, such as “Dripping water can wear away the stone”, “Yu Gong moves mountains” and so on. The idiom “Dripping water can wear away the stone” means that constant dripping water can wear through the stone. As long as you have perseverance and work hard, things will succeed in the end. Similarly, the tale of "Yu Gong moves mountains" shows how perseverance can help with great accomplishments. It is a fable by Liezi, a thinker during the Warring States Period. Yu Gong and his descendants faced two mountains that blocked the road. They did not fear hardship and insisted on digging the mountains, and finally the Emperor of Heaven helped to move the mountains away. This story shows the perseverance of the people in ancient China.

Similar Chinese proverbs such as "Where there is a will, there is a way", "There is nothing difficult in the world, as long as people have the determination", etc. all show that we must persevere to overcome difficulties, which would inspire future generations to keep working for a long time for their dreams. Sometimes, even if the expected result cannot be fully achieved, action and persistence will definitely make things progress. This is similar to the western proverb "Perseverance Prevails".

注 释 Notes

Yǒu zhì zhě shì jìng chéng.
有 志 者 事 竟 成 。

Where there is a will, there is a way.

"有志者事竟成"是一句汉语谚语，出自《后汉书》，意思是有志向的人做事一定会成功，启发后人要拼搏奋斗，在困难中勇往直前。

"有志者事竟成" is a Chinese proverb that comes from the book *Houhanshu*. It means that people with aspirations will succeed in doing things, and that would inspire future generations to work hard and move forward courageously despite difficulties.

学而时习之 Practice Makes Progress

(一) 选词填空 (Choose the correct words for the blanks)

A. 凉快　　B. 耐心　　C. 放弃　　D. 严格

1. 老师对我很(　　　)，但这是为了我好。

2. 即使研究汉语再难，安娜也不会（　　）。

3. 最近，天气越来越（　　）了。

4. 安娜没有（　　）练习长跑。

（二）连词成句（Form sentences with the words given）

1. 态度　　的　　积极　　她　　很好

____

2. 放松身心　　可以　　听音乐　　的时候　　跑步

____

3. 有信心　　我　　更　　让　　鼓励　　他的

____

4. 可惜　　现在　　太　　了　　放弃　　你

____

（三）阅读理解（Read and choose the right option）

安娜在上海读博士三个月了，她觉得读博士比读硕士难多了。张教授说她积极的态度很好，鼓励她不要放弃。安娜觉得张教授虽然严格，但是他的鼓励也让她更有信心坚持下去。

1. 根据上文，安娜觉得读博士比读硕士怎么样？（　　）

A. 有趣　　B. 简单　　C. 难　　D. 无聊

2. 张教授的鼓励让安娜怎么样？（　　）

A. 很累　　B. 更有信心　　C. 开心　　D. 很忙

（四）口语练习（Speaking task）

请用下面的词，向你的小组介绍一位老师，并选择两个句子写下来。

A. 严格　　B. 鼓励

C. 尊重　　D. 态度

1. ____________________

2. ____________________

（五）看图写句子（Look at the pictures and make sentences with the words given）

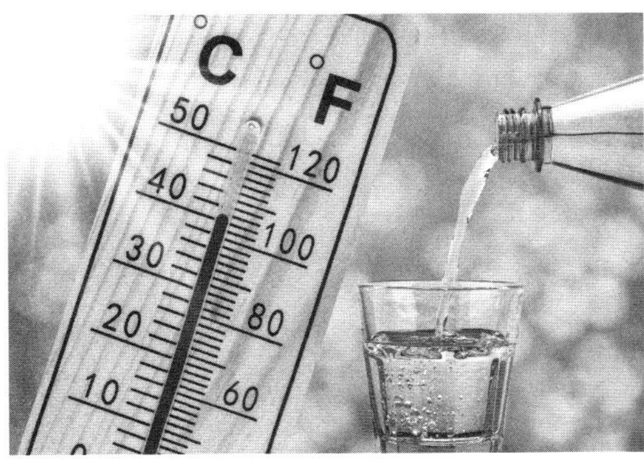

温度

____

流行

____

吃惊

____

压力

____

第四课　无论是否成功，我都会接受

学习目标 Learning Objectives

1. 掌握工作面试相关词汇

Understand the vocabulary related to job interviews

2. 运用“无论……，都……”表示结果不变或无法避免

Use “无论……，都……” to emphasize inevitable results

课文 1 Text 1

在咖啡厅

李明：安娜，你今天怎么不高兴啊？

安娜：别提了。今天刚收到消息，我申请“上海市优秀博士生”奖学金失败了。好失望啊！

李明：没关系。也许下次申请你就成功了。

安娜：已经没有下次了，留学生只能申请一次。

李明：是吗？但无论怎么样，都不要影响心情。

安娜：好的，我要继续努力，也许还有其他机会。

李明：没错！我记得你是个特别自信的女孩，无论是否成功，你都一直十分积极。

安娜：可是最近我压力有点大，你和欧文都工作了，我却还是个学生。

李明：如果你在经济方面有压力，我可以给你介绍工作。

安娜：好的，谢谢！我得找个留学生能做的工作。

李明：没问题，找到了我联系你。

词汇 1　Vocabulary 1

1	提	tí	*v.*	to mention
2	申请	shēnqǐng	*v.*	to apply for
			n.	application
3	奖学金 *	jiǎngxuéjīn	*n.*	scholarship
4	失败	shībài	*v.*	to be defeated; to fail
			adj.	unsuccessful
5	失望	shīwàng	*v.*	to feel disappointed 失：to lose　望：hope
			adj.	disappointing
6	也许	yěxǔ	*adv.*	perhaps; maybe
7	无论	wúlùn	*conj.*	regardless of; no matter
8	自信	zìxìn	*n.*	self-confidence
			adj.	self-confident
9	是否	shìfǒu	*adv.*	whether; whether or not

课文 2　Text 2

到教育公司面试

安娜：经理，您好！我是来面试兼职老师的。我叫安娜，这是我的申请表格。

经理：原来你就是安娜呀？你好！李明经常提到你。你是他的女朋友吧？

安娜：您误会了，我不是他的女朋友。我们以前是同学。

经理：哦，不好意思。那你来我们公司想当汉语老师还是英语老师？

安娜：我都行。无论汉语还是英语，我上课都没问题。

经理：很好，你非常符合我们的要求！但你是兼职老师，每个月只能拿百分之五十的工资，不过干得好的话有奖金。

安娜：好的，无论有没有奖金，我都会好好干！

经理：行！你先回去等消息，还有几个人要面试。你把申请表格留在这儿，有结果了我会马上通知你。

安娜：好的，谢谢您！

词汇 2 Vocabulary 2

1	教育	jiàoyù	*v.*	to educate
			n.	education
2	兼职	jiānzhí	*n.*	part-time job (HSK5 Word)
3	表格	biǎogé	*n.*	form; table
4	原来	yuánlái	*adj.*	former; original
			adv.	It turns out that…
5	误会	wùhuì	*v.*	to misunderstand
			n.	misunderstanding
6	行	xíng	*adj.*	capable; competent; okay
7	奖金	jiǎngjīn	*n.*	reward; bonus
8	干	gàn	*v.*	to do one's job
9	通知	tōngzhī	*v.*	to inform
			n.	notice; notification

课文 3　Text 3

做一个诚实的人

上周一，我和李明去了一个咖啡厅聊天，他提出要帮我介绍兼职工作。结果周五下午，我就去了他介绍的教育公司面试。

去之前，我很紧张，因为这是我第一次参加工作面试。我专门请了一个有教育公司实习经验的同学帮我练习。同学说我的普通话很标准，到教育公司当中英文老师都行。她还告诉我，面试一定得诚实回答问题。

这次面试很顺利，不过面试中发生了一个小误会。经理竟然以为我是李明的女朋友，我马上解释我和李明只是同学。经理好像是李明的朋友，然而我不想让她由于这种误会而降低面试标准。我宁可得不到这份兼职，也要做一个诚实的人。

面试结束后，经理说她很喜欢我的诚实。她认为无论是做汉语老师还是英语老师，我在教学方面都没问题。不过，面试结果要到下周才出来，我还得耐心等通知。

上次申请"上海市优秀博士生"奖学金虽然失败了，但我努力过了。这次面试，我对于结果一点都不紧张，无论是否成功，我都会接受。

词汇 3　Vocabulary 3

1	诚实	chéngshi	*adj.*	honest
2	专门	zhuānmén	*adv.*	specially
3	标准	biāozhǔn	*n.*	criterion; norm
			adj.	standard
4	发生	fāshēng	*v.*	to happen; to take place

5	解释	jiěshì	*v.*	to explain
6	然而	rán'ér	*conj.*	nevertheless; however
7	降低	jiàngdī	*v.*	to reduce; to bring down
8	宁可	nìngkě	*adv.*	would rather (HSK5 Word)

语 法 Grammar

无论……，都……（No matter...）

"无论……，都……"表示不管出现什么情况，结果都是一样的，或前提条件不同，结果也不变，强调没有例外。"无论"是连词，表示在任何条件下结果或结论都不会改变，常用于"无论……，都/也……"结构。"无论"后面可以是表示选择关系的并列成分，也可以是表示任指的疑问代词。例如：

"无论……" means "no matter...". The conjunction "无论" means the result or conclusion will not change under any circumstances, and it is used in the structure "无论……, 都/也……". It can be followed by a coordinate alternative, or an interrogative pronoun that refers to anybody or anything. For example,

1. 无论有没有奖金，安娜都会好好工作。
2. 无论做汉语老师还是英语老师，安娜都没问题。
3. 无论是否成功，安娜都会积极接受。

走近中国 A Touch of China

儒家交友之道

中国有句俗话叫"在家靠父母，出门靠朋友"，表明朋友在中国人的心目中占有非常重要的地位。传统儒学把朋友关系列为五种人伦关系之一，可见儒家对朋友关系的重视。

儒家的交友之道主要有如下几个方面：

第一，重视交友。儒家主张“以文会友，以友辅仁”，认为交友既能相互切磋学问，又能促进彼此的道德修养，并认为有益的快乐有三种，其中之一即是多交好朋友。

第二，谨慎交友。孔子主张多交益友而不交损友，明确指出判断好朋友和坏朋友的标准：朋友要正直，不暴躁易怒；朋友要宽容，不优柔寡断；朋友要博学多才，不花言巧语。孔子还主张以志同道合交友，以道义交友而非以利交友，即在交友上强调以道义的契合为基础，在大是大非面前坚持原则，互相支援，才合乎交友之道。

第三，待友有道。首先，孔子主张待友以“信”为根。“与朋友交，言而有信”，与朋友交往，答应的事就守信用，做到对朋友诚实无欺，这是最根本的原则。其次，以“恕”为怀。要求做人要谦虚谨慎，严于律己，宽于责人。朋友之间难免会发生一些龃龉与不和，如果朋友之间互相谅解，对朋友关系发展有极大意义。宽宏大度、谦虚待友，可使友情长存不衰。最后，以“和”为贵。一方面，孔子认为朋友之间的“和”不是简单的盲从附和、绝对的同一，而是“和而不同”，强调朋友之间在保持个性差异基础上和谐统一。另一方面，朋友之“和”是明辨是非、讲原则的“和”。

儒家尚交友、慎择友、善待友的交友之道，有其深刻的人生哲理和鲜明的人文向度，历久弥新。在当今社会，儒家交友之道对于改善社会风气，建立和谐的人际关系，以及世界多元文化的并存共进，具有重要的现实意义。

The Confucian Way of Making Friends

There is a Chinese saying “Rely on parents at home and friends when going out”, which shows that friends occupy a very important position in the minds of Chinese people. Traditional Confucianism lists friendship as one of the five types of human relations, which shows that Confucianism attaches great importance to friendship.

The Confucian way of making friends has the following main aspects:

First, attach importance to making friends. Confucianism advocated “to make friends through literature, and to develop benevolence with friends". They believe that friends can not only learn from each other, but also promote each other's moral cultivation. They also believe that there are three kinds of beneficial happiness, one of which is to make good friends.

Second, make friends carefully. Confucius advocated making more beneficial friends rather than making bad friends, clearly pointing out the criteria for judging good friends and bad friends: friends must be upright and not irritable; friends must be tolerant and not indecisive; friends must be knowledgeable and talented, and mustn't speak untruthfully. Confucius also advocated making friends with like-minded people and friendship should be based on morality rather than profit. That is to say, when making friends, it emphasizes the basis of moral harmony, adheres to principles and supports each other in the face of major issues of right and wrong, and it is the way to make friends.

Third, treat friends in a proper way. First of all, Confucius advocated treating friends with "faith" as the root. "Make friends by keeping your word", and keep your promises when you interact with friends, and be honest with your friends. This is the most fundamental principle. Secondly, take "forgiveness" as a bosom. Friends are to be humble and prudent, strict in self-discipline, and lenient in responsibility. It is inevitable that there will be some discord between friends. If friends understand each other, it is of great significance to the development of friendship. To be magnanimous and to treat friends humbly can make the friendship last forever. Finally, "harmony" is the most important thing. On the one hand, Confucius believes that the "harmony" between friends is not simply blind obedience and absolute identity, but "harmony with difference", emphasizing harmony and unity between friends on the basis of maintaining individual differences. On the other hand, the "harmony" of friends is the "harmony" that distinguishes right from wrong and stresses principles.

The Confucian way of making friends, choosing friends carefully, and treating friends kindly, has its profound philosophy of life and distinctive humanistic orientation, which will last forever. In today's society, the Confucian way of making friends has important practical significance for fostering social atmosphere, establishing harmonious interpersonal relationships, and for the coexistence of multiple cultures in the world.

注 释 Notes

Rújiā
儒家

Confucianism

儒家是孔子创立、孟子发展，为后代推崇，至今仍有一定生命力的学术流派。儒家起源于中国，提倡“仁”，是流传至其他东亚国家的一种文化主流思想与哲理体系。

Confucianism is an academic school that was founded by Confucius and developed by Mencius. It is admired by future generations and still has a certain vitality. Confucianism originated in China and advocated “benevolence”, which is a mainstream cultural ideology and philosophy system that has spread to other East Asian countries.

学而时习之 Practice Makes Progress

（一）选词填空（Choose the correct words for the blanks）

A. 申请　　B. 误会　　C. 诚实　　D. 是否

1. 上次的奖学金（　　），安娜失败了。
2. 无论（　　）成功，安娜都会接受。
3. 安娜是一个非常（　　）的人，不说假话。
4. 经理（　　）了，她以为安娜是李明的女朋友。

（二）连词成句（Form sentences with the words given）

1. 专门请了　同学　我　帮忙　一个

____

2. 她　诚实　是　一个　人　的

____

3. 申请　这里　把　你　表格　留在

____

4. 通知　结果　有　马上　就　你　了

____

(三) 阅读理解 (Read and choose the right option)

安娜去了李明介绍的教育公司面试。面试的过程中，经理误会她是李明的女朋友。安娜跟经理解释他们只是硕士时候的同学，因为她不希望经理降低面试标准。安娜觉得做诚实的人很重要。

1. 根据上文，面试的过程中经理怎么了？（　　）

A. 生气　B. 开心　C. 开会　D. 误会

2. 安娜觉得什么很重要？（　　）

A. 有趣　B. 专业　C. 诚实　D. 认真

(四) 口语练习 (Speaking task)

请用下面的词，向你的小组介绍一次自己的面试经历，并选择两个句子写下来。

A. 诚实　B. 解释
C. 申请　D. 标准

1. ______________________________

2. ______________________________

（五）看图写句子（Look at the pictures and make sentences with the words given）

申请

____

通知

____

自信

____

教育

____

第五课　难道就我一个人不知道吗

学习目标 Learning Objectives

1. 掌握爱情话题相关词汇

Understand the vocabulary related to the topic of love

2. 运用“难道……吗？”进行反问

Use “难道……吗？” to ask rhetorical questions

课文 1 Text 1

在宿舍

同学：安娜，上次面试有结果了吗？

安娜：结果还没出来，不过很感谢你帮我练习。

同学：咱们之间不用客气。面试顺利吗？

安娜：还行。你猜面试时那个经理问了我什么？

同学：面试一般会问与专业、经验有关的信息。难道你遇到了什么不礼貌的问题吗？

安娜：也不算不礼貌。那个经理问我是不是李明的女朋友。

同学：哈哈，也许李明介绍你的时候给她留下了这样的印象吧。

安娜：啊？可是李明从来没有向我表示过他喜欢我。

同学：也许他不敢直接告诉你吧，男孩子都害怕被拒绝。我们所有人都知道他喜欢你。

安娜：难道就我一个人不知道吗？

同学：差不多！他现在已经工作了，身边肯定有很多不错的同事。要是他跟别人约会了，你可别后悔啊。

安娜：我才知道他喜欢我。我得约他出来聊一聊。

词汇 1　Vocabulary 1

1	猜	cāi	*v.*	to guess
2	难道	nándào	*adv.*	indicating an interrogating tone of rhetorical question
3	礼貌	lǐmào	*n.*	manners; politeness
			adj.	polite
4	表示	biǎoshì	*v.*	to express; to mean
5	敢	gǎn	*aux.*	dare
6	直接	zhíjiē	*adj.*	direct
7	拒绝	jùjué	*v.*	to decline; to reject
8	所有	suǒyǒu	*adj.*	all of; every
9	约会	yuēhui	*v.*	to go on a date 约：to make an appointment 会：meeting

课文 2　Text 2

约李明见面

李明：安娜，不好意思，我来晚了。你等了很久吧？

安娜：没事，我也才到不久。你礼拜天不用加班吧？

李明：不加班。我听教育公司的王经理说你的面试很顺利。

安娜：嗯。不过，今天我约你出来，不是说面试的事情。

李明：好的，那你想说什么？

安娜：李明，我特别感谢生命中有你和欧文这样的好朋友出现。每次和你们聊天，我都能忘掉烦恼。

李明：你怎么了，安娜？

安娜：你有很多优点，但是我现在读博太累了，还不想考虑找男朋友的事情。

李明：我明白。我是很喜欢你，尤其是你的自信和积极的态度很吸引我。但你不要有压力，我刚参加工作比较忙，还不想找女朋友。

安娜：好的，我也不是一直都很自信和积极。我也有很多缺点，你发现之后也许就不会喜欢我了。

李明：我难道会因为你有缺点就不喜欢你了吗？即使你有缺点，我还是会喜欢你的。这次你拒绝我没关系，我们还是好朋友。如果你在上海遇到什么困难，还可以找我帮忙。

安娜：谢谢你，李明。我很感动。

词汇 2 Vocabulary 2

1	礼拜天	lǐbàitiān	*n.*	Sunday 礼拜：week　天：day
2	生命	shēngmìng	*n.*	life
3	出现	chūxiàn	*v.*	to appear
4	掉	diào	*v.*	to drop; to lag behind
5	烦恼	fánnǎo	*n.*	trouble
			adj.	worried; distressed
6	优点	yōudiǎn	*n.*	merit; advantage 优：excellent　点：point
7	考虑	kǎolǜ	*v.*	to consider
8	吸引	xīyǐn	*v.*	to attract
9	缺点	quēdiǎn	*n.*	shortcoming; weakness 缺：deficiency　点：point

课文 3　Text 3

我心中的爱情

读博后，我就搬进了学校的博士生宿舍，这样去图书馆更方便。礼拜六，我在宿舍遇到了之前帮我练习面试的同学。她提醒我李明喜欢我很久了，而且所有同学都知道。

但是，我还不确定自己与他之间是友谊还是爱情。我想对自己和他都诚实一点。礼拜天，我就约李明出来吃饭，礼貌地拒绝了他。

其实，这次我拒绝李明，自己也挺难受的。我心中的爱情是经常陪在男朋友身边，一起过浪漫而有趣的生活。然而，这些我都无法做到，我感觉没时间陪他。我读博士压力很大，也许还要一边工作一边学习。他刚工作也很忙，我们能在一起的时间很少。

李明有很多优点，读硕士的时候他一直耐心地帮助我和欧文适应中国的生活。我们在一起学习的时候很开心，但是工作后肯定会有不少烦恼。如果只接受他的帮助，却无法陪着他解决烦恼，也不合适。

吃完饭，他先走了，我感觉他有点伤心。李明说我们还是好朋友，让我有困难时一定要找他。但我感觉这已经不可能了。我已经拒绝了他，难道还要再联系他吗？在没有确定是爱情之前，我宁可自己解决困难，也不想再去麻烦他。

词汇 3　Vocabulary 3

1	爱情	àiqíng	*n.*	love
2	提醒	tíxǐng	*v.*	to remind
3	确定	quèdìng	*v.*	to be sure
			adj.	definite
4	难受	nánshòu	*adj.*	uncomfortable; unwell; not feeling physically relaxed; sad 难：difficult　受：to bear

5	陪	péi	*v.*	to accompany
6	浪漫	làngmàn	*adj.*	romantic
7	有趣	yǒuqù	*adj.*	interesting
8	无	wú	*v.*	to lack
9	伤心	shāngxīn	*adj.*	sad; heart-broken 伤：to injure　心：heart

语 法 Grammar

难道 + 反问句（*Nandao* + Rhetorical Question）

"难道……吗？" 可以表示反问，"难道" 是副词，后面加反问的内容，此类问句不需要回答。例如：

Rhetorical questions use the form of a question to emphasize a point, which often do not require an answer. "难道" is used as a marker to form this kind of questions. "难道……吗?" can be used to ask rhetorical questions in Chinese. For example,

1. 难道就我一个人不知道吗？
2. 我难道会因为你有缺点就不喜欢你了吗？
3. 我已经拒绝了他，难道还要再联系他吗？

走近中国 A Touch of China

中国的情人节

农历七月初七是中国传统的情人节——七夕节，它已有 2000 多年的历史，来源于织女和牛郎的浪漫传说。

在中国民间传说中，织女是玉皇大帝的女儿之一。她对天庭的平凡生活感到厌倦，于是下凡与凡人牛郎相爱。不幸的是，天庭反对他们在一起，并用一条巨大的银河将他们永远分开。一群喜鹊被这对夫妻的爱情所感动，它们在每年的农历七月初七这一天，在银河上搭成一座桥，让牛郎和织女相见。后来，天庭允许这对恋人在每年的农历七月七日在“鹊桥”相会。

七夕节给予了情侣表达感激与爱意的机会。像西方的情人节一样，很多中国情侣会在七夕节约会，交换精心准备的礼物，享受丰盛的晚餐，等等。七夕节给中国的大街小巷带来了浪漫的气息，情侣们凝视夜空，寻找织女星和牵牛星，体味着美丽传说中织女和牛郎之间的真挚情感，表达相互间的爱慕之情。据不完全统计，唐宋时期七夕主题的诗词达近400首。有杜甫的《牵牛织女》：“牵牛出河西，织女处其东。万古永相望，七夕谁见同。”宋代秦观的那一句“金风玉露一相逢，便胜却人间无数”，更是道出了男女相思离别的人间苦乐。

每年公历五月二十日，是中国的新式情人节——“520节”，即“我爱你节”。由于汉语中有大量的同音和近音字，当代中国出现了一种用数字代替谐音汉字的网络俚语现象，产生了“520（我爱你）节”。很多中国人选择在五月二十日表白求婚，甚至注册结婚。在七夕节和五月二十日这样的日子里，商家也会推出各种各样的活动吸引年轻人进行消费。中国当代社会的情人节文化也变得更加多元化。

Chinese Valentine's Day

The seventh day of the seventh month of the Chinese lunar calendar is the traditional Chinese Valentine's Day—Qixi Festival. It has a history of more than two thousand years and is derived from the romantic legend of the Weaver Girl and the Cowherd.

In Chinese folklore, the Weaver Girl is one of the daughters of the Jade Emperor. She was bored with the ordinary life of heaven, so she went down and fell in love with the normal Cowherd. Unfortunately, the heavenly court opposed their being together and used the huge Milky Way to separate them forever. A group of magpies was moved by the couple's love. They built a bridge across the Milky Way on the seventh day of the seventh month of the lunar calendar, allowing the Cowherd and the Weaver Girl to meet each other. Later, the heavenly court allowed the lovers to meet at the "Magpie Bridge" on the seventh day of the seventh lunar month of each year.

The Qixi Festival gives couples an opportunity to express their gratitude and love. Like Valentine's Day in the West, many Chinese couples will exchange carefully prepared gifts, enjoy a great dinner and so on during the Qixi Festival. It brings a romantic atmosphere to the streets and alleys of China. The lovers gaze at the night sky, looking for the Vega and Altair, and appreciate the sincerity between the beautiful legend, and express their mutual affection. According to incomplete statistics, there are nearly 400 poems on the theme of Qixi in the Tang and Song Dynasties. There is Du Fu's "The Vega and Altair": "The Altair is in the west of Milky Way, and Vega in the east. People say they can meet in Qixi, but who really witnessed it?" Qin Guan of the Song Dynasty said, "When Autumn's Golden Wind embraces Dew of Jade, all the other love scenes on earth fade." It also speaks of the human sufferings and joys of parting and lovesickness between men and women.

Every year on May 20th in the Gregorian calendar, it is China's new-style Valentine's Day: "520 Festival", i.e. "I Love You Festival". Due to the large number of homophones and near-phonetic characters in Chinese, a phenomenon of Internet slang that uses numbers to replace near-phonetic Chinese characters has appeared in contemporary China, resulting in the "520 (I Love You) Festival". Many Chinese choose to confess their love on May 20th, or even register for marriage. On days such as Qixi Festival and May 20th, businesses will also launch various activities to attract young people to consume. The culture of Valentine's Day in contemporary Chinese society has thus been more diversified.

学而时习之 Practice Makes Progress

（一）选词填空（Choose the correct words for the blanks）

A. 猜　　B. 优点　　C. 提醒　　D. 难道

1. 同学（　　）安娜，李明很喜欢她。
2. （　　）你没听说过李小龙吗？
3. 虽然他有很多（　　），但是我不喜欢他。

4. 你（　　）面试的时候，经理说了什么？

（二）连词成句（Form sentences with the words given）

1. 难道　你　知道　这件事　不　吗

____

2. 优点　他的　我　吸引　很

____

3. 她的生活　出现　中　爱情　了

____

4. 考虑　她　现在　不　男朋友　找

____

（三）阅读理解（Read and choose the right option）

同学提醒安娜，李明喜欢安娜很久了。安娜约李明出来聊天，说自己还不想找男朋友。虽然李明有很多优点，但是安娜读博士太累了，所以拒绝了李明。李明离开的时候好像有一点伤心。

1. 根据上文，安娜为什么拒绝李明？（　　）

A. 太累了　B. 太忙了　C. 太自信了　D. 太无聊了

2. 李明离开的时候怎么样？（　　）

A. 很开心　B. 有点高兴　C. 有点累　D. 有点伤心

（四）口语练习（Speaking task）

请用下面的词，向你的小组介绍一个朋友，并选择两个句子写下来。

A. 优点　B. 缺点
C. 有趣　D. 礼貌

1. ______________________________

2. ______________________________

（五）看图写句子（Look at the pictures and make sentences with the words given）

约会

____

烦恼

____

难受

____

浪漫

____

第六课　虽然被批评了，但我特别感动

学习目标 Learning Objectives

1. 掌握交通事故和看病相关词汇

Understand the vocabulary related to traffic accidents and seeing a doctor

2. 运用被动句强调不如意事情的发生

Use passive sentences to emphasize the negative impact of an event

课文 1 Text 1

在医院遇到张阿姨

欧文：护士，您好！请问医院里有可以打电话的地方吗？

护士：护士站那边有电话。呀！你是欧文吧？

欧文：我是欧文。请问您是？

护士：我是张阿姨，你的房东王教授的妻子。你怎么来医院了？

欧文：原来是张阿姨呀！第一次见您穿护士服，没有认出您来。今天早上下小雨，我骑自行车的时候不小心撞到出租车了。

护士：撞到哪里了？严重吗？

欧文：为了保护电脑，我的右胳膊摔伤了，自行车和手机也摔坏了。

护士：出租车司机呢？撞了你，应该在医院陪着你才对。

欧文：张阿姨，您别误会！不是我被他撞了，而是他的车被我撞了。这件事情责任在我。司机师傅非常友好，不仅接受了我的道歉，还马上开车把我送到医院来了。

护士：怎么没看到他？

欧文：我让他先走了。他陪我做完了检查，结果没什么严重的问题。

护士：好吧。我现在带你去护士站打电话吧，你记得电话号码吗？

欧文：我看一下电脑。我把所有重要的号码都提前存到电脑里了。

护士：也许你电脑里存了很多重要资料，但将来要是再遇到这样的情况，一定要先保护自己。生命只有一次，千万要注意安全。

欧文：您说得对，以后我一定小心。谢谢您！

词汇 1 Vocabulary 1

1	撞	zhuàng	*v.*	to run into; to bump into (HSK5 Word)
2	严重	yánzhòng	*adj.*	serious; severe
3	保护	bǎohù	*v.*	to protect; to safeguard
4	胳膊	gēbo	*n.*	arm
5	摔 *	shuāi	*v.*	to fall; to drop and break
6	责任	zérèn	*n.*	duty; responsibility
7	道歉	dàoqiàn	*v.*	to apologize 道：to say　歉：apology
8	资料	zīliào	*n.*	material; resource; data (HSK5 Word)
9	将来	jiānglái	*n.*	future
10	情况	qíngkuàng	*n.*	situation; state of affairs

课文 2 Text 2

给李想打电话

李想：喂，您好！这里是美国大使馆。

欧文：您好！我是欧文。请问李想在吗？

李想：欧文，我就是李想，你到现在都没来上班，给你打电话一直占线。是不是发生了什么事情？我们很担心。

欧文：是这样的：今天早上我骑车去上班，不小心撞上了路边的出租车，胳膊摔伤了，当时就疼得抬不起来了。

李想：你现在怎么样了？没事吧？

欧文：没事。医生说，胳膊伤得不太严重，不用住院。但是因为胳膊很疼，恐怕我还得在家休息几天。

李想：人没事，我们就放心了。我先帮你请个假，等你回到家，最好还是自己给大使馆发个正式邮件解释一下原因。

欧文：好的，谢谢！那明天的会议怎么办呢？需要我把翻译好的材料发给你吗？

李想：我正准备告诉你，受到天气的影响，回北京的所有航班全部推迟了，要参会的几位同事估计都无法赶回北京。经过商量，这次会议改成线上举行了。

欧文：太好了，这样我就可以在家参会了。

李想：如果你能参会，当然是最好的。但是你胳膊很疼的话，估计翻译的时候无法记下所有关键信息。这次我帮你翻译吧！

欧文：嗯，现在写字和打字确实比较困难，那这次就麻烦你帮我翻译。太感谢了！

李想：同事之间不用客气，你在家好好休息。

词汇 2　Vocabulary 2

1	占线	zhànxiàn	*v.*	to be busy (telephone line) 占：to occupy　线：string; line
2	抬	tái	*v.*	to lift; to raise; (of two or more persons) to carry
3	恐怕	kǒngpà	*v.*	to worry
			adv.	I'm afraid that...

4	受到	shòudào		to receive (praise, an education, punishment, etc.)
5	全部	quánbù	*n.*	all; the whole; the entire 全：whole; entire　部：part
6	估计	gūjì	*v.*	to estimate
7	商量	shāngliang	*v.*	to talk over; to discuss
8	举行	jǔxíng	*v.*	to hold (a meeting, ceremony, etc.)
9	确实	quèshí	*adj.*	reliable; true
			adv.	indeed; truly

课文 3 Text 3

安全第一

时间过得真快！我实习结束成为美国大使馆的正式翻译快三个月了。本来工作和生活都挺顺利的，前几天我却把自己的胳膊摔伤了。

那天早上，广播里说："今天有中雨转小雨，交通会受影响。请注意交通安全。"周末我刚买了一辆新自行车，又看到当时窗外确实只是小雨，于是我还是决定骑新车去上班。

我一边骑车一边考虑第二天会议的翻译工作，结果一个没注意就撞上了停在路边的出租车。我的右胳膊摔伤了，手机和新买的自行车也都摔坏了。虽然我不是故意的，但到底还是给被我撞到的出租车司机带来了麻烦。我向司机师傅道了歉，并获得了他的原谅。虽然我的胳膊伤得不太严重，医生还是建议我请假在家休息几天。

在医院我幸运地遇到了张阿姨，她正好是这家医院的护士。当时，我正急着找电话打给大使馆说明情况。张阿姨批评我，即使电脑里的资料很重要，也不应该只想到保护电脑却没保护好自己，并提醒我生命只有一次，安全第一。虽然被批评了，但我却特别感动，张阿姨确实很关心我。

接着，张阿姨带我去护士站打了电话。李想告诉我第二天的会议改成线上举行了，我仍然可以在家参会。不过，我胳膊摔伤了，恐怕不方便写字和打字，这次就先麻烦李想帮我做翻译工作了。

等回到家，休息了一会儿，我冷静地回忆起早上的事情，真的感觉有点害怕，幸亏我只是摔伤了胳膊。如果真的发生了什么严重的事情，爸爸妈妈会多么难受和伤心啊！张阿姨提醒得对，安全第一，将来我一定要注意。

词汇 3　Vocabulary 3

1	广播	guǎngbō	*n.*	broadcast; broadcasting
			v.	to broadcast; to be on the air
2	故意	gùyì	*adv.*	deliberately; on purpose
3	获得	huòdé	*v.*	to obtain; to gain
4	原谅	yuánliàng	*v.*	to excuse; to forgive; to pardon
5	幸运	xìngyùn	*adj.*	fortunate; lucky (HSK5 Word)
			n.	good fortune; good luck
6	说明	shuōmíng	*v.*	to explain; to illustrate; to indicate; to prove
			n.	explanation; directions; caption
7	批评	pīpíng	*v.*	to criticize
8	冷静	lěngjìng	*adj.*	calm; cool-headed
9	回忆	huíyì	*v.*	to recall

语　法　Grammar

"被"字句小结（Summary of the *Bei*-sentence）

在汉语中，"被"可以用来表示被动。"被"字句的结构为"主语 + 被 + 宾语 + 动词 + 其他成分"，主语为动作的受事者，宾语为动作的施事者。"被"后面的宾语可以省略。有时，"叫"和"让"可以替代"被"。在意义被动句中，受事是主语，不强调施事，"被"可以省略。例如：

In Chinese, a sentence with "被" can express the passive voice, its structure being "S + *Bei* + O + Verb", in which the subject is the patient of the action and the object is the agent. The object following "被" can be left out. Sometimes, "被" can be replaced by "叫" and "让". "被" needs to be omitted in some particular passive sentences when the patient of the action serves as the subject. For example,

1. 欧文的胳膊（被）摔伤了。
2. 回北京的所有航班全部（被）推迟了。
3. 虽然被批评了，但欧文却特别感动。

走近中国 A Touch of China

中国"重人贵生"的思想

中国哲学并不像西方哲学流派那样注重对宇宙与客观世界的探讨，而是更加关注人的存在及其生命价值等问题。中国道家对生死问题有着比较深刻的阐述，尊重生命、贵生养生。《庄子》中"生"字出现了 250 多次，而"死"字也出现了 170 多次。

中国道家思想讲究道法自然，站在宇宙的高度去思考人的生命意义与价值，强调"重人贵生"，倡导人的生命价值高于一切。《道德经》指出"道大，天大，地大，人亦大"，将"人"放在了与"道""天""地"同等重要的地位。老子提出："名与身孰亲？身与货孰多？得与亡孰病？"他认为对于个体来说，名利得失都是外在的、无足轻重的，只有生命才是最重要的。这也启示后人，以生命和身体为代价去追求名利的行为是不明智的。《太平经》也认为天地之间"人命最重""寿为最善"，敬重生命是人类的本性。中国儒家思想也有类似的生命观。孔子认为"天地之大德曰生"，强调重生、贵人、孝亲、修德、保身等内容。

中国"重人贵生"的文化在当代中国对民生的重视中得以继承。在新冠疫情爆发后，中国人民重视生命安全，自觉居家隔离，出行必戴口罩做好防护，这不仅是为了保护自己，也是对他人生命健康负责的表现。另外，中国已经进入老龄化社会或者出现了老龄化社会现象，道家的“重人贵生”思想也启发当代社会更加注重老龄人群的生命安全与养老福利建设。

China's Philosophy in Valuing People and Lives

Chinese philosophy does not focus on the exploration of the universe and the objective world like western philosophical schools, but pays more attention to issues such as human existence and the value of life. Chinese Taoists have a relatively profound exposition on the issue of life and death, respecting life and maintaining health. In the book *Zhuangzi*, the word for "life" appeared more than 250 times, and the word for "death" appeared more than 170 times.

Chinese Taoist thought pays attention to learning from the nature, thinking about the meaning and value of human life from the perspective of the universe. Taoism emphasizd "valuing people and lives", and advocated that the value of human life is above all else. The book *Dao De Jing* pointed out: Dao is great, heaven is great, earth is great, human beings are great, and human beings are placed in a very important position. Lao Tzu asked "Which one is more important: the fame, the body, or the materials? Which one is worse, the gains or the death?" He believed that for an individual, fame, gain and loss are external and insignificant, and only life is the most important. This also enlightens later generations that it is unwise to pursue fame and fortune at the expense of life and health. The book *Tai Ping Jing* also believed that "life is the most important" and "longevity is the best". Respecting life is the nature of mankind. Chinese Confucianism also has a similar view of life. Confucius believed that "the great virtue of heaven and earth is life", emphasizing the value of people and life, filial piety, cultivation of morals, and self-preservation etc.

China's culture of valuing people and life is inherited in contemporary China's emphasis on people's livelihood. After the outbreak of the Covid-19, the Chinese people attach importance to life and safety, stayed at home, and always wore masks for protection when traveling. This is not only to protect themselves, but also to be responsible for the lives and health of others. In addition, China has gradually stepped into a phase of having too many elderly people. Taoism's "valuing people and lives" has also inspired contemporary society to pay more attention to the life safety and pension benefits of them.

学而时习之 Practice Makes Progress

（一）选词填空（Choose the correct words for the blanks）

A. 批评　　B. 原谅　　C. 回忆　　D. 保护

1. 他（　　）了事情的过程，觉得很害怕。
2. 为了（　　）电脑，欧文的胳膊摔伤了。
3. 欧文虽然被（　　）了，但是很感动。
4. 对不起，你能（　　）我吗？

（二）连词成句（Form sentences with the words given）

1. 严重　不　的　我　伤

____

2. 我们　会议　明天的　一下　商量

____

3. 原谅　获得　我　了　他的

____

4. 航班　推迟　的　恐怕　明天　要

____

（三）阅读理解（Read and choose the right option）

欧文上班的时候不小心撞到了路边的出租车，胳膊摔伤了。虽然不严重，但是需要在家休息几天。他在医院的时候遇到了张阿姨，她提醒欧文安全第一，不能为了保护电脑却不保护自己。欧文给李想打了电话，李想说这次先帮欧文翻译。

1. 根据上文，欧文撞到了什么？（　　）

A. 公交车　B. 出租车　C. 自行车　D. 人

2. 李想这次先帮欧文做什么？（　　）

A. 骑车　B. 开车　C. 翻译　D. 休息

（四）口语练习（Speaking task）

请用下面的词，向你的小组介绍一次被批评的经历，并选择两个句子写下来。

A. 批评　　B. 原谅
C. 回忆　　D. 恐怕

1. ______________________________

2. ______________________________

（五）看图写句子（Look at the pictures and make sentences with the words given）

获得

____

估计

____

道歉

____

广播

____

第七课　这个词语究竟是什么意思

学习目标 Learning Objectives

1. 掌握汉语教学相关词汇

Understand the vocabulary related to Chinese teaching and learning

2. 运用“究竟……”进行提问或强调事实

Use “究竟……” to intensify a question or emphasize a fact

课文 1 Text 1

王经理来听课

安娜：王经理，谢谢您来听我的课。这是我的第一节汉语课，请您多多指导。

经理：不客气！指导谈不上，你上课很自然，词语也讲得很不错。我只提一点建议，就是有的词语你还可以解释一下它在实际生活中的意思。比如你在白板上写的这个“火”字，除了指自然中的火，还可以表示“流行”的意思。

安娜：好的，谢谢您！我在这方面还有很多要提高的地方。很多词语在实际生活中究竟是什么意思，我还要多向同事们学习。

经理：这很好！上汉语课是一门艺术，因为很多汉语词语都有不同的意思，要讲清楚不容易。

安娜：是的，我发现与教英语比起来，教汉语难得多。

经理：没错！但我对你有信心，你一定能把汉语课上好。有机会我会再来听你的课。

安娜：谢谢您的指导与鼓励！

词汇 1　Vocabulary 1

1	节	jié	*m.*	section
2	指导	zhǐdǎo	*v.*	to guide; to coach (HSK5 Word)
3	自然	zìrán	*n.*	the nature world
			adj.	natural
			adv.	naturally; certainly
4	词语	cíyǔ	*n.*	word
5	实际	shíjì	*adj.*	real; actual
6	火	huǒ	*n.*	fire
			adj.	popular
7	指	zhǐ	*v.*	to point at; to refer to
8	究竟	jiūjìng	*adv.*	on earth
9	艺术	yìshù	*n.*	art

课文 2　Text 2

在办公室

同事：安娜，欢迎你来我们公司当汉语老师。你的第一节课上得怎么样？

安娜：尽管王经理说很不错，但我知道这是她客气。我教学中有一些错误，经理好心没有全部都指出来。

同事：有错误是正常的，你不要因此怀疑自己的教学能力。

安娜：好的。我还是得多研究汉语词语，这样才能帮助学生更准确地理解每节课的词语。

同事：嗯，一些重点词语，你可以上网查一下它的用法，让学生提前预习课文。实际上，很多中国老师也不清楚一些词语究竟是什么意思，也经常需要使用词典。

安娜：好的。我以前教过英语，感觉比教汉语容易多了。

同事：究竟教英语难还是教汉语难，每个老师的感觉都不一样。不过，课上得多了，自然会一天比一天容易的。

安娜：好，要是有与汉语词语有关的问题，我可以找你请教吗？

同事：当然没问题，我们可以一起讨论！

安娜：太感谢了！

词汇 2 Vocabulary 2

1	错误	cuòwù	*n.*	error; mistake
2	正常	zhèngcháng	*adj.*	normal
3	因此	yīncǐ	*conj.*	therefore; so
4	怀疑	huáiyí	*v.*	to suspect
5	准确	zhǔnquè	*adj.*	accurate
6	理解	lǐjiě	*v.*	to understand; to comprehend
7	重点	zhòngdiǎn	*n.*	focus; key point 重：heavy 点：point
8	请教	qǐngjiào	*v.*	to ask for guidance (HSK6 Word)
9	讨论	tǎolùn	*v.*	to discuss; to talk over

课文 3　Text 3

第一次教汉语

上个礼拜一，王经理通知我面试通过了，一周后可以去公司上课。这个好消息让我非常兴奋。为了上好第一节汉语课，我准备了一个礼拜。

第一次上课前我特别紧张，去了好几趟厕所。王经理来听了我的课，说我上课很自然。然而，我知道自己对一些汉语词语的理解还不够准确。我与王经理讨论了一些词语在生活中的意思，比如，"火"还有生气和受欢迎的意思。经理指着白板说，中国人经常说一本书或一部电影很火。

听课结束后，王经理提到，与学英语的学生相比，来我们公司学汉语的学生数量太少了。今年暑假，学英语的人数是学汉语的十倍，实际上这种情况已经很久了。因此，在教汉语的同时，我还有一个任务，就是去学校和对面的公司发广告，吸引更多的人寒假来我们公司上汉语课。

我计划这学期结束后在学校调查一下究竟有多少刚来上海的留学生，希望他们中有人想来我们公司学汉语。

其实，我不担心学生数量少的问题。现在已经不缺少想学汉语的学生了，而是缺少能教好汉语的老师。我一定要努力做好博士研究，同时也要做一个专业而有趣的老师，吸引更多的人来学汉语。

词汇 3　Vocabulary 3

1	兴奋	xīngfèn	*adj.*	excited; exciting
2	厕所	cèsuǒ	*n.*	toilet
3	数量	shùliàng	*n.*	quantity; amount
4	倍	bèi	*m.*	times; -fold

5	同时	tóngshí	*n.*	same time
			conj.	at the same time
6	任务	rènwu	*n.*	task; mission
7	对面	duìmiàn	*n.*	the opposite side
8	调查	diàochá	*v.*	to investigate; to survey
			n.	investigation;survey
9	缺少	quēshǎo	*v.*	to lack; to be short of

语 法 Grammar

究竟 + 目标问题（*Jiujing* + Targeted Questions）

在汉语中，“究竟”可以用来询问具体信息，后面一般可以加是非疑问小句、选择疑问小句或特殊疑问小句等。有时，“究竟”还有“毕竟”的意思。例如：

“究竟” can be used to intensify a question, aiming at finding out a specific piece of information. Sometimes, “究竟” can mean “after all”, which is similar to “毕竟”. For example,

1. “火”字在这里究竟是什么意思？
2. 究竟是汉语难教还是英语难教，每个人的看法不一样。
3. 安娜究竟是李明推荐来的，课上得真好！

走近中国 A Touch of China

儒家教育思想

儒家思想是中国传统文化的核心，其中教育方面包含了教育目的、学习方法、师生关系等内容，我们称之为儒家教育思想。儒家教育思想以孔子哲学思想为源头，在之后发展的过程中逐渐丰富完善，不仅对中国教育史产生了深远影响，也是世界教育史的宝贵遗产。

儒家在教育哲学和教学方法领域有很多极有价值的主张。第一个主张是“有教无类”：一方面，从教育提供者而言，对教学对象不应该有等级贵贱之分，应该为所有人提供教育平等与公平；另一方面，从受教育者而言，不管什么人都可以接受教育，教育能弥补学生先天智力等方面的不足，帮助其成长。第二个主张是“因材施教”：孔子注意到了教学对象的差别化特点，提出了应该根据学生资质进行针对性教学的原则。儒家学者朱熹曾评价这一点说：“夫子教人各因其材”，继承与深化了因材施教的主张。第三个主张是“学思并重”，孔子认为“学而不思则罔，思而不学则殆”，意思是：只读书而不思考，死记硬背，不能深刻理解意义，会陷入迷茫；只思考而不去认真学习，不能有效利用知识，只能是脱离知识与实际的空想。这告诉学习者只有把学习和思考结合起来，将理论联系实践，才能做到真正的进步。这些主张与西方的“Education for All”“分层区别化教学”“在用中学”等教育理念相似。

另外，儒家教育思想还提出教师应该具备“学而不厌，诲人不倦”的精神，在学习过程中不应满足，在教学过程中不应厌倦。孔子认为“后生可畏”，提出了“教学相长”的概念，明确教与学可以相互促进，学生可以启发教师精益求精。因此，不管是学生还是教师，都要坚持学习，这与西方“Lifelong Learning”的终身学习理念不谋而合。

Confucian Educational Thought

Confucianism is the core of traditional Chinese culture, and covers educational aspects which include educational purposes, learning methods, teacher-student relations, etc. We call this Confucian educational thought. It is based on Confucian philosophy and is gradually enriched in subsequent developments. It not only has a profound impact on the history of Chinese education, but also is a valuable heritage of world education history.

Confucianism has proposed many extremely valuable claims in terms of educational philosophy and teaching methods. The first claim is "Education without discrimination". On the one hand, from the perspective of education providers, there should be no distinction among students with different backgrounds, and education should be provided for equality and fairness for all. On the other hand, all are entitled the right to education, so education can make up for students' innate deficiency of intelligence and other aspects to help them develop. The second proposition is "Teach students in accordance with their aptitude". Confucius noticed the different characteristics of learners and put forward the principle that tailored instruction should be carried out according to students' levels. Confucian scholar Zhu Xi once commented on this point: "The master Confucius teaches people according to their aptitude", inheriting and deepening the idea of teaching students with differentiation. The third proposition is "Combining learning and thinking". Confucius believed that "learning without thinking is worthless, thinking without learning is perilous". It means that studying books by rote memorization is not helpful to understand the meaning deeply, resulting in confusion. If people only think but don't study hard, the knowledge cannot be used effectively, the thinking can only be a fantasy divorced from reality. This tells learners that only by combining learning and thinking, and combining theory with practice, can they make real progress. These propositions are similar to the Western educational concepts such as "Education for All", "Differentiated teaching" and "Learning by doing".

In addition, Confucian educational thought also proposes that teachers should possess the spirit of "Never feel tired of learning and teaching", and should not be satisfied in the process of learning and teaching. Confucius believed that "the young generation has nothing to fear" and put forward the concept of "teaching and learning benefit each other". Teaching and learning can promote each other, and students can inspire teachers to strive for excellence. Therefore, both students and teachers must persist in learning, which coincides with the Western educational concept of "Lifelong Learning".

学而时习之 Practice Makes Progress

（一）选词填空（Choose the correct words for the blanks）

A. 词语　　　B. 兴奋　　　C. 究竟　　　D. 理解

1. 他（　　）喜不喜欢你？
2. 很多（　　）的意思，我还不是很清楚。
3. 我得到了那个工作，我太（　　）了！
4. 她是我最好的朋友，她非常（　　）我。

（二）连词成句（Form sentences with the words given）

1. 不要　你　怀疑　的　能力　自己

____

2. 欢迎　火　意思　还有　受　的

____

3. 十倍　学汉语的　人数　学英语的　是

____

4. 艺术　一门　是　上　课　汉语

____

（三）阅读理解（Read and choose the right option）

安娜开始去教育公司当兼职汉语老师了。经理觉得安娜的课上得不错，给她提了一些建议。安娜觉得教汉语很有趣，之后会多学习汉语词语在生活中的意思。经理还给了安娜一个任务，就是吸引更多的人到公司来学汉语。

1. 根据上文，安娜觉得教汉语怎么样？（　　）

A. 很无聊　　B. 很难　　C. 很有意思　　D. 很忙

2. 安娜还有一个什么任务？（　　）

A. 教英语　　B. 写文章　　C. 吸引学生　　D. 当经理

（四）口语练习（Speaking task）

请用下面的词，向你的小组介绍一次汉语课，并选择两个句子写下来。

A. 词语　　B. 究竟
C. 因此　　D. 错误

1. ____________________

2. ____________________

（五）看图写句子（Look at the pictures and make sentences with the words given）

火

____

讨论

____

调查

____

厕所

____

第八课　实际情况与他们说的相反

学习目标 Learning Objectives

1. 掌握环境保护相关词汇

Understand the vocabulary related to protecting the environment

2. 运用“……，相反，……”陈述对立的情况

Use “……，相反，……” to state the opposite situation

课文 1 Text 1

在宿舍

安娜：黄丽，快起床吧！今天天气很好，我们要不要出去走走？

黄丽：好啊！你看到我的眼镜了吗？我不戴眼镜什么都看不清。

安娜：我记得你好像昨晚放在厕所里了，我去拿给你。

黄丽：好的。我肚子好饿，咱们先去餐厅吃早餐，然后去学校对面的公园转转吧。

安娜：行，正好把垃圾倒掉。

黄丽：好的。我看外面太阳很大，要不要带把伞？

安娜：为什么要带伞？难道出门不是为了晒太阳吗？

黄丽：哈哈，跟你相反，我出门的时候喜欢打太阳伞、戴太阳镜。这样可以保护皮肤，不会被晒黑。

安娜：好吧，哈哈！难怪我经常看到有女孩在晴天的时候打伞，原来她们

是为了不被晒黑。

黄丽：是的，中国人觉得女生皮肤白一点更好看。

安娜：那我们国家正好相反，我们认为皮肤颜色深一点更有吸引力。

黄丽：为什么呀？

安娜：这说明你经常旅行或运动，比较健康。还有人专门花钱去晒黑呢！

黄丽：是吗？看来我们对美的标准不太一样。真有趣！

词汇 1 Vocabulary 1

1	眼镜	yǎnjìng	*n.*	glasses; spectacles
2	戴	dài	*v.*	to wear; to put on
3	肚子	dùzi	*n.*	stomach; belly
4	倒	dào	*v.*	to throw away
5	晒	shài	*v.*	to bask in the sunshine (HSK5 Word)
6	相反	xiāngfǎn	*adj.*	opposite
			conj.	on the contrary
7	皮肤	pífū	*n.*	skin
8	难怪	nánguài	*adv.*	no wonder (HSK5 Word)
9	深	shēn	*adj.*	deep

课文 2 Text 2

在公园

安娜：我发现在上海，到处都能看到这样不同颜色的垃圾桶。

黄丽：是的，上海从去年就开始进行“垃圾分类”了。

安娜：对垃圾进行分类管理特别好，垃圾中很多材料都是可以再用的，比如干净的纸盒与塑料瓶什么的。

黄丽：没错。垃圾分类以后，由垃圾引起的污染也减少了。

安娜：在垃圾分类方面，上海做得真好！希望中国其他城市在发展经济的同时，也能这么重视自然环境的保护。

黄丽：实际上中国很多地方都在进行垃圾分类。我父母每天都坚持在家里用各种颜色的分类垃圾桶呢！

安娜：啊，那太好了！我们在宿舍也应该这样。保护地球是我们每个人的责任！

黄丽：是呀，那咱们回去的时候顺便去超市买一些分类垃圾袋吧。

安娜：好主意！将来宿舍里的各种垃圾咱们一定要认真进行分类。

词汇 2　Vocabulary 2

1	进行	jìnxíng	*v.*	to carry out; to conduct
2	分类 *	fēnlèi	*v.*	to classify
3	管理	guǎnlǐ	*v.*	to manage
4	由	yóu	*prep.*	from
5	引起	yǐnqǐ	*v.*	to bring; to cause
6	污染	wūrǎn	*n.*	pollution
			v.	to pollute
7	减少	jiǎnshǎo	*v.*	to reduce; to decrease
8	各	gè	*pron.*	each; every
9	地球	dìqiú	*n.*	the Earth

课文 3　Text 3

"有色眼镜"不能戴

这个周末，上海天气特别好，我和黄丽一起去逛了学校对面的公园。公园的环境好极了，到处都可以看到不同颜色的分类垃圾桶，十分方便。黄丽告诉我，她的家人即使不在上海，也一样重视各种生活垃圾的分类。我觉得中国的环保工作做得越来越好了。

来中国之前，我身边有不少人习惯戴着“有色眼镜”来看中国和亚洲。都二十一世纪了，他们还认为只有自己的国家很富，以为中国和许多亚洲国家仍然很穷，而且污染严重。然而，他们的这些想法都是错误的。

来中国之后，我发现这里的实际情况与他们所说的相反，中国的发展不仅速度快，而且质量好，尤其是这几年，各种云经济、云教育都非常成功。我来中国三年多了，去过许多省市，看到的都是蓝天白云，污染也越来越少了。我的眼睛看到的一座座山、一条条河都能证明中国在自然环境保护与管理方面的努力。

如果戴着“有色眼镜”看世界，我们看到的东西往往是不准确的。我很幸运能够来到中国，看到真实的中国究竟是什么样的。等我回去，一定要提醒家人和朋友不要戴“有色眼镜”，要去了解真实情况，而不是只看电视与报纸。

在回学校的路上，我和黄丽去超市买了一些不同颜色的垃圾袋，准备认真地进行垃圾分类。我们都深深相信，无论是谁，都有责任保护这个地球！

词汇 3 Vocabulary 3

1	亚洲	Yàzhōu	*n.*	Asia
2	世纪	shìjì	*n.*	century
3	富	fù	*adj.*	rich
4	许多	xǔduō	*num.*	many; a lot of; lots of
5	穷	qióng	*adj.*	poor; poverty-stricken
6	云	yún	*n.*	cloud
			adj.	online
7	座	zuò	*m.*	measure word for buildings or mountains
8	证明	zhèngmíng	*v.*	to prove; to testify
9	真实	zhēnshí	*adj.*	true; real (HSK 5 Word)

语　法　Grammar

……，相反，……（...，in contrast，...）

在汉语中，“……，相反，……”可以陈述对立的情况。注意，“相反”的前后需要使用两个逗号，间隔两个分句。例如：

“……, 相反, ……” can be used to state the opposite situations. “相反” is normally used after the first clause, between two commas, to introduce the second clause. For example,

1. 你喜欢打伞，相反，我喜欢晒太阳。
2. 外国人喜欢皮肤颜色深，相反，中国人喜欢皮肤白一点。
3. 他以为这里污染很严重，相反，这里的环境非常好！

走近中国　A Touch of China

中国的“天人合一”自然观

“天人合一”是中国传统哲学中对人与自然关系的精辟概括，认为自然与人是一个密切相关的整体，会相互影响、相互作用，强调人与自然应当和谐相处、共存共荣。其基本内涵包括如下四个层面：

一是敬畏自然，视自然与人为一体。人与自然具有内在统一性，是息息相通的一体，处于不可分割的联系中。人是自然的一部分，人要敬畏自然。人类对大自然的伤害最终会伤及人类自身。人类善待自然，也就是善待自己。

二是尊重自然，视自然为人类之家。“天人合一”思想最深刻的含义之一，就是承认自然界具有生命意义，具有自身的内在价值。人类是大自然长期孕育的产物，是自然之子。大自然为人类的生存和发展提供了全部需要，就像家长一样，不仅给孩子生命，还供给孩子吃穿住行，为孩子提供成长的空间。因此，人类应该像尊重父母一样尊重大自然。

三是顺应自然，视自然为人类之师。我国古代的农耕文明注重师法自然，不夺农时。自然规律是客观存在的，人应顺应自然，不能违背自然规律，要“效法自然”。对自然界的开发利用要“适时”而“有节”，不能乱砍伐、乱捕杀。君王要学习天地日月的无私品德，公平、公正地对待所有人，国家才能长治久安。

四是保护自然，视自然为人类之友。人与万物具有平等性，人与自然是一种互利共生的朋友关系。出于维护自身生存和道义原则的需要，人肩负着保护自然界的责任。因为动植物也是有生命、有感情的，应将万物看作自己的朋友，对大自然要有不忍之心、恻隐之心，并加以体恤、爱护。

“天人合一”思想包含的古典生态智慧具有极为重要的当代价值，是解决当下资源约束趋紧、环境污染严重、疫情频发、生态系统退化等生态危机的一剂良药。

Harmony between Nature and Man: a Chinese Perspective

“Harmony between nature and man” is an incisive summary of the relationship between man and nature in traditional Chinese philosophy. It believes that nature and man are a closely related whole that will influence and interact with each other. It emphasizes that man and nature should live in harmony, coexist and prosper together. Its basic connotation includes the following four levels:

The first one is to respect and regard nature and man as one. Man and nature have an inherent unity, that are closely interlinked, and are in an inseparable connection. Man is a part of nature, and man must respect nature. Human harm to nature will eventually harm human beings. Human beings are kind to nature, that is to be kind to human beings themselves.

The second is to respect nature as the home of mankind. One of the most profound connotations of the idea of “Harmony between man and nature” is to recognize that the natural world has the meaning of life and has its own intrinsic value. Human beings are the long-term conceived products of nature and are the children of nature. Nature provides all the needs for human survival and development. Just like parents, they not only gives children life, but also provides children with food, clothing, shelter and space for growth. Therefore, human beings should respect nature like their parents.

The third is to conform to nature and regard nature as the teacher of mankind. China's ancient agricultural civilization paid attention to learning from nature and following nature's timings. The laws of nature exist objectively, and people should conform to nature, not violate the laws of nature, and imitate nature. The development and utilization of the natural world must be timely and regularly, and should not be cut down indiscriminately. The emperor must learn the selfless character of the world, and treat all people fairly and justly, so that the country can maintain long-term stability.

The fourth is to protect nature and regard nature as a friend of mankind. Man and everything are equal, and man and nature are a mutually beneficial and symbiotic friendship. Out of the need to maintain their own survival and moral principles, people shoulder the responsibility of protecting the natural world. Because animals and plants also have lives and emotions, you should regard everything as your own friends, as well as you must have intolerance and compassion toward nature, as well as be sympathetic and loving.

The classical ecological wisdom contained in the idea of "Harmony between nature and man" has extremely important contemporary value. It is a good solution to the current ecological crises such as tightening resource constraints, serious environmental pollution, frequent epidemics and ecosystem degradation.

注 释 Notes

Yǒusè yǎnjìng
有色 眼镜

Prejudice

"有色眼镜"是一个汉语成语，意思是用含有个人主观色彩的眼光看待人或事物，启示后人不要对他人有偏见，应该一视同仁。

"有色眼镜" is a Chinese idiom, which means to look at people or things with a personal subjective perspective. It inspires future generations not to prejudice against others and everyone should be treated equally.

学而时习之　Practice Makes Progress

（一）选词填空（Choose the correct words for the blanks）

A. 眼镜　　B. 亚洲　　C. 世纪　　D. 污染

1. 中国的（　　）越来越少了，到处都是蓝天白云。
2. 出太阳的时候，我喜欢戴太阳（　　）和打伞。
3. 他去过许多（　　）国家和地区旅游。
4. 二十一（　　）了，很多人都开上了汽车。

（二）连词成句（Form sentences with the words given）

1. 污染　　引起　　垃圾　　少了　　的

____

2. 情况　　相反　　实际　　说的　　与他们

____

3. 分类　　垃圾　　上海　　进行　　了　　开始

____

4. 晒　　不　　太阳　　我　　喜欢　　特别

____

（三）阅读理解（Read and choose the right option）

安娜没来中国之前，她的很多朋友以为中国的污染很严重，但实际情况正相反。中国的环境越来越好了，很多城市已经开始进行垃圾分类管理了。安娜在中国三年多了，她去了很多省市，发现到处都是蓝天白云。这证明了中国在环境保护方面的努力。

1. 根据上文，中国环境怎么样？（　　）

A. 很多污染　　B. 越来越好了　　C. 不好　　D. 越来越差

2. 安娜发现中国到处都是什么？（　　）

A. 工厂　　B. 商店　　C. 蓝天白云　　D. 学校

（四）口语练习（Speaking task）

请用下面的词，向你的小组介绍一个城市，并选择两个句子写下来。

A. 许多　　B. 污染
C. 管理　　D. 相反

1. ______________________________

2. ______________________________

（五）看图写句子（Look at the pictures and make sentences with the words given）

地球

____

眼镜

____

污染

____

富

____

第九课　平平安安才是真，健健康康就是福

学习目标 Learning Objectives

1. 掌握家庭关系与出差相关词汇

Understand the vocabulary related to relationships among family members and going on business trips

2. 正确运用名词、量词、形容词、动词（包括离合词）的重叠

Use the reduplication of nouns, measure words, adjectives and verbs, including separable words, correctly and appropriately

课文 1 Text 1

父亲的爱

欧　文：张阿姨，一到周末您就给我做这么多好吃的，真是太麻烦您了。

张阿姨：一点儿都不麻烦，给家人准备好吃的是我的爱好。我还担心会打扰你周末休息呢。

欧　文：当然不会啦！王教授怎么没在家？

张阿姨：他去学校了。他的学生遇到了一些研究方面的问题，要向他请教。

欧　文：我同事是王教授以前的学生，听他说王教授是学校最受学生欢迎的老师之一。王教授确实从心底关心他的学生们。

张阿姨：是呀！让我烦恼的是他不知道怎么表达对自己孩子的关心。他经常问我儿子的情况，却很少直接和儿子对话。

欧　文：虽然都是满满的关心和爱，但是父亲表示关心的方式有时候和母亲不一样，不过我相信你们的孩子一定能理解的。

张阿姨：确实是这样。比如，当时儿子选择出国留学的时候，我是反对的，我希望他留在北京读研究生，但他父亲支持他出国。虽然意见不一样，但他知道我们都是爱他的。

欧　文：他能做出自己的决定，您和王教授心里一定感到很骄傲。

张阿姨：嗯，他从小到大一直是我们的骄傲。欧文，你没见过我儿子吧？给你看看他和同学们的照片，你猜猜哪个是他？

欧　文：好啊！是这个个子高高的男生吗？他长得很像王教授。

张阿姨：哈哈，是的。他小时候眼睛大大的，小脸圆圆的，很像我。长大后越来越像他爸爸了。对了，欧文，还有四五个星期就要过春节了。如果你没有其他安排的话，我们想邀请你跟我们一起过春节。

欧　文：我还从来没有在中国人家里过过春节呢。谢谢您！我非常愿意。

词汇 1　Vocabulary 1

1	父亲	fùqin	*n.*	father
2	打扰	dărăo	*v.*	to disturb; to bother; to trouble
3	底	dĭ	*n.*	bottom; base; end (of the month, year, etc.)
4	对话	duìhuà	*v.*	to have a dialogue or conversation
5	满	măn	*adj.*	full; filled; packed
			v.	to fill; to reach the limit
			adv.	fully; completely; quite
6	方式	fāngshì	*n.*	way; manner; style; mode (HSK5 Word)
7	反对	fănduì	*v.*	to fight against; to oppose; to be opposed to; to disagree with
8	支持	zhīchí	*v.*	to be in favor of; to support
9	意见	yìjian	*n.*	opinion; idea; complaint

10	骄傲	jiāo'ào	*adj.*	proud; conceited
			n.	pride; a person or thing worth being proud of

课文 2 Text 2

准备出差

欧文：李想，我刚收到电子邮件，大使馆安排我们两个明天去厦门出差。

李想：我也接到通知了。原来安排去出差的同事昨天生病住院了，大使今天早上才决定改成我们俩，所以这次出差来得比较突然。你的胳膊怎么样了？可以出差吗？

欧文：没有问题，我的胳膊已经完全好了。

李想：明天厦门将举办一场重要的中美经济文化交流活动，大使要参加，需要我们做现场翻译。到时候现场会有许多记者，所以要求翻译一定要准确。

欧文：我在现场翻译方面没有太多经验。我需要提前准备什么呢？

李想：关于这场活动的中英文材料，我已经进行了整理，等一下发给你。你可以稍微准备准备，按照我整理的顺序进行阅读，比较重要的内容需要提前记住，例如用红笔写的就是一些关键信息。当然，你也可以按照自己习惯的方式进行准备。

欧文：这是我第一次出差，我现在的心情真是既激动又紧张。

李想：放轻松点，不要有太大压力。

欧文：好的，我一定认真阅读，好好准备。

李想：明天的航班是早上六点的，你下班回去后简单收拾收拾就早些休息吧。

欧文：我会的。有你这么一位有经验的同事指导我、帮助我，实在是太幸运了，谢谢你！

李想：不用客气！有什么问题，尽管来问我。

词汇 2　Vocabulary 2

1	出差	chūchāi	*v.*	to go on an official or business trip
2	举办	jǔbàn	*v.*	to conduct; to hold
3	场	chǎng	*m.*	measure word for sporting or recreational activities; measure word for exams, rain, snow, etc.
			n.	large place used for a specific purpose; stage; scene (of a play)
4	交流	jiāoliú	*v.*	to communicate; to exchange
5	现场	xiànchǎng	*n.*	spot; site; work field; the scene (of a crime, accident, etc.) (HSK6 Word)
6	顺序	shùnxù	*n.*	sequence; order
7	阅读	yuèdú	*v.*	to read
8	内容	nèiróng	*n.*	content; substance
9	例如	lìrú	*v.*	for example; for instance; such as

课文 3　Text 3

我想家了

上个周末，张阿姨谈到她儿子小时候的样子，让我也回忆起自己小时候的生活。一件件有趣的事情、一场场难忘的旅行、一段段快乐的回忆，就好像发生在昨天。

春天的时候，爸爸和妈妈会带着我去郊区的森林散散步，看看美丽的大自然，偶尔还会爬爬树。一到暑假，我们全家就会去海边旅游，晒晒太阳，游游泳。秋天到了，我们就去参观附近的葡萄园，爸爸妈妈会尝尝新出的葡萄酒，而我就只能吃吃新鲜的葡萄了。下雪的时候，爸爸会带我到院子里堆堆雪人，烤烤火，妈妈就会在厨房里做好吃的蛋糕。到了周末，爸爸会带我去爬爬山，踢踢球，妈妈会陪我聊聊天，听我讲讲学校里发生的故事。现在回忆起来，小时候的生活是多么幸福啊，每天都开开心心的，好像没有任何烦恼。

我来中国之后，虽然和父母之间的距离远了，但家人之间的感情还是那么好，我相信父母永远都是这个世界上最关心自己的人。只不过，现在我和父母联系得不像以前那么多了，一方面是因为我长大了，有了自己的工作和生活；另外一方面是工作之后，来自各个方面的压力比以前增加了许多，如果告诉父母，除了增加他们的烦恼，没有其他作用。

但是张阿姨的话提醒了我，父母一定也很想了解我在中国的真实情况，不仅是开心的事情，还有我的烦恼和压力。比如我上次摔伤胳膊了，妈妈肯定会说："平平安安才是真，健健康康就是福。我们不在你身边，你要照顾好自己呀！"

我想家了！我想听听父母的声音，看看父母的样子。等这次出差回来，我一定要给他们打个电话，好好聊一聊最近的事情，关于是否留在中国工作，我正好也想听听他们的看法。

词汇 3 Vocabulary 3

1	偶尔	ǒu'ěr	*adv.*	occasionally; once in a while
2	幸福	xìngfú	*n.*	happiness; well-being 幸：good fortune; luck 福：blessings
			adj.	happy; blessed
3	感情	gǎnqíng	*n.*	emotion; sentiment; affection; feelings between two persons
4	永远	yǒngyuǎn	*adv.*	forever
			n.	eternity
5	另外	lìngwài	*pron.*	other; another
			adv.	besides; moreover
			conj.	furthermore; in addition

6	来自	láizì	v.	to come from
7	增加	zēngjiā	v.	to raise; to increase 增：to increase; to expand　加：to add
8	平安	píng'ān	adj.	safe and sound; well; without mishap (HSK5 Word)
9	看法	kànfǎ	n.	perspective; view; opinion

语　法　Grammar

重叠（Reduplication in Chinese）

汉语中有很多重叠现象，如动词重叠、形容词重叠、量词重叠等。动词重叠常表示短暂迅速的动作或尝试，形容词重叠常表示强调事物的特征，量词重叠常表示所有事物都没有例外。例如：

In Chinese, verbs, adjectives and measure words are often reduplicated, to indicate a short/quick action, an attempt, or without exception, and "every" to the noun that follows, depending on the context. When reduplicating single character verbs like "看", "一" can be inserted (e.g. "看看, 看一看"). When reduplicating two-character verbs (e.g. "收拾收拾"), "一" is no longer needed. For example,

1. 你下班回去后收拾收拾就早些休息。
2. 平平安安才是真，健健康康就是福！
3. 一件件有趣的事情，就好像发生在昨天。

走近中国　A Touch of China

中国人的家庭观

家庭是中国文化中的基础概念，中国是个孝亲爱亲的国度。中国人注重血缘关系和亲情伦理，家永远是中国人情感汇聚的核心。家的观念根深蒂固地存在于每个中国人的心里，与中华文化中的“孝道”观念紧密相关。

“孝”是中国社会公认的道德观念，是中国文化伦理精神的本质。著名学者梁漱溟先生曾经在《中国文化要义》中提出，中国家庭文化就是“孝的文化”。儒家文化讲究“仁”，仁者爱人。孝是对父母及长辈的仁爱表现，是“仁”的根本。每年春节，大量在外务工的中国人都要返回家乡，因为故乡有亲人和家。在中国及受到中华文化影响的亚洲国家，家庭中的长者受到晚辈的尊敬，晚辈受到长辈的照拂。在传统社会中，尤其是那些生活在农村的大家庭，常有四世同堂或更多代家人住在一起的情况。即使在现代家庭中，许多祖父母也和他们的孩子住在一起，帮助抚养孙辈。这与西方文化的独立家庭观非常不同。

为了解决人口过多但资源不足的问题，中国在 20 世纪 70 年代末实行了独生子女政策，提倡一个家庭只生一个孩子。这一政策使中国当代社会的家庭结构产生了变化。随着中国人口和资源之间矛盾的逐步缓解，该政策已于 2016 年进行了调整，中国的核心家庭单位也由三口之家向四口甚至更多人口之家转变。不管中国未来社会及家庭结构怎样变迁，“孝”作为仁爱之心及伦理道德的根源和最具特色的中国文化元素是永远不会变的。尽管目前中国年轻人也逐渐开始接受一些西方家庭文化的观念，但传统的中国孝道家庭价值观将会持续存在。

Chinese View of Family

Family is a basic concept in Chinese culture, and China is a country of filial piety and close family relationships. Chinese people pay attention to kinship and family ethics, and family is always the core of Chinese emotions. The concept of family is deeply ingrained in the heart of Chinese and is closely related to the concept of “filial piety” in Chinese culture.

“Filial piety” is a recognized moral concept in Chinese society and the essence of Chinese cultural ethics. The famous scholar Liang Shuming once pointed out in *The Essentials of Chinese Culture* that Chinese family culture is the “culture of filial piety”. Confucian culture emphasizes “benevolence”, and the benevolent loves others. Filial piety is a benevolence to parents and elders, and it is the foundation of "benevolence". When Spring Festival comes, a large number of Chinese working afar have to return to their hometowns because they have relatives and families there. In China and some Asian countries influenced by Chinese culture, the elderly in the family are respected by the younger generation, and the younger generations are taken care of by the elderly. In traditional societies, especially those large families living in rural areas, there are often four and sometimes more generations living together. Even in modern families, many grandparents live with their children and help raise their grandchildren. This is very different from the independent family value of western culture.

In order to solve the problem of overpopulation but insufficient resources, China implemented the one-child policy at the end of the 1970s, advocating only one child per family. This policy has brought about changes in the family structure of contemporary Chinese society. With the gradual easing of the contradiction between population and resources, this policy has been adjusted in 2016. China's nuclear family unit has also changed from a family of three to a family of four or more. No matter how the social and family structure changes in China, "filial piety", as the root of benevolence ethics and the most distinctive Chinese cultural element, remains the same. Although Chinese young people are gradually accepting some western concepts of family culture, the traditional Chinese family values of filial piety will continue to exist.

学而时习之　Practice Makes Progress

（一）选词填空（Choose the correct words for the blanks）

A. 感情　　B. 永远　　C. 交流　　D. 反对

1. 他们的（　　）很好，计划马上结婚。
2. 她的爸爸妈妈十分（　　）她跟他结婚。
3. 她说会（　　）记得小时候开心的事情。
4. 明天大使馆会举办一场中外文化（　　）活动。

（二）连词成句（Form sentences with the words given）

1. 永远　　人　　是　　父母　　关心　　我的

______

2. 他　　准确　　要求　　翻译　　我　　一定要

______

3. 骄傲　　心里　　他　　非常　　感到

______

4. 受　　王教授　　在学校　　欢迎　　很

______

（三）阅读理解（Read and choose the right option）

欧文房东的妻子是张阿姨，她做饭非常好吃。张阿姨说虽然王教授很少直接跟儿子对话，但实际上非常爱儿子。张阿姨谈起了儿子小时候的样子，让欧文也回忆起自己小时候的生活，一件件有趣的事情，就好像发生在昨天。

1. 根据上文，王教授跟儿子交流怎么样？（　　）

A. 很多　　B. 很直接

C. 非常多　　D. 很少直接对话

2. 欧文回忆起了什么？（　　）

A. 中学　　B. 大学　　C. 小时候的生活　　D. 小学

（四）口语练习（Speaking task）

请用下面的词，向你的小组介绍一张照片，并选择两个句子写下来。

A. 回忆　　B. 幸福

C. 永远　　D. 另外

1. ____

2. ____

（五）看图写句子（Look at the pictures and make sentences with the words given）

满

____

感情

____

阅读

____

出差

____

第十课　演员们表演得精彩极了

学习目标 Learning Objectives

1. 掌握考试与演出相关词汇

Understand the vocabulary related to exams and performances

2. 正确运用各种补语结构表示程度、数量、状态等

Use various complement structures to indicate degree, quantity, status, etc., correctly and appropriately

课文 1 Text 1

在宿舍复习

黄丽：安娜，还剩一周就是期末考试了，你复习得怎么样了？

安娜：最近兼职有点忙，没怎么复习。而且我也不知道博士生的期末考试应该怎么复习。

黄丽：听说博士生的期末考试跟硕士生不一样，不考填空、判断、阅读理解这样的汉语知识题。估计张教授会让大家写一篇讨论汉语教学的文章交给他。

安娜：太好了！我通过做兼职汉语教师，对教学有很多新的看法，正好想和老师交流呢。

黄丽：那很棒！我一直在学习理论知识，还没实践过，没什么与汉语教学有关的内容可写。

安娜：那我跟你交流一下实践经验，咱们一起复习吧。

黄丽：好的，太感谢了！

安娜：不用客气，我的也不是标准答案，只是我自己对教学的看法。

黄丽：这正好是我缺少的东西，对我来说很有帮助！

词汇 1　Vocabulary 1

1	剩	shèng	*v.*	to be left over; to remain
2	填空	tiánkòng	*v.*	to fill in the blanks
3	判断	pànduàn	*v.*	to judge
4	知识	zhīshi	*n.*	knowledge
5	篇	piān	*m.*	measure word for articles or papers
6	交	jiāo	*v.*	to make friends; to hand over; to submit
7	理论	lǐlùn	*n.*	theory (HSK5 Word)
8	实践	shíjiàn	*v.*	to practise (HSK5 Word)
			n.	practice
9	答案	dá'àn	*n.*	answer

课文 2　Text 2

期末考试

安娜：黄丽，是你的手机在响吗？还是谁在敲门啊？

黄丽：是我的手机，你快醒醒！今天是期末考试，千万不能迟到。

安娜：你的手机响声比敲门声还大！我昨晚睡得太晚了，刚才还在做梦呢。

黄丽：我知道你复习得很晚，已经帮你把毛巾和牙膏弄好了。快点起来，我们还得去吃早餐呢。

安娜：谢谢！我马上起床。

黄丽：我昨晚紧张得睡不着，现在还很困。但是咱们宁可少睡半个小时，也要早点去教室做好考试准备。

安娜：好的！我梦到张教授没让我们写文章，还是考了原来的选择题、判断题什么的。

黄丽：无论考什么题，我都不担心。咱们已经复习得很仔细了。

安娜：是的，我们不仅复习了理论知识，还交流了实践经验。

黄丽：没错！考完了咱们下午去逛街吧？

安娜：好啊！

词汇 2 Vocabulary 2

1	响	xiǎng	*v.*	to ring; to sound
			adj.	loud
2	敲	qiāo	*v.*	to knock
3	醒	xǐng	*v.*	to wake up
4	梦	mèng	*n.*	dream
			v.	to dream
5	毛巾	máojīn	*n.*	towel
6	牙膏	yágāo	*n.*	toothpaste
7	弄	nòng	*v.*	to do; to manage (informal)
8	困	kùn	*adj.*	sleepy
			v.	to trap; to be in trouble
9	仔细	zǐxì	*adj.*	careful

课文 3 Text 3

放寒假了

上周五，汉语专业的博士生们参加了期末考试。考试前，我与黄丽一起认真地复习了一周，不仅复习了汉语知识点，还互相交流了汉语教学经验。考试那天早上，幸亏黄丽帮我弄好了牙膏，要不然我可能会迟到。她是我在上海交的第三个好朋友！

这场考试竟然没考原来常考的填空题、判断题、阅读理解题等。张教授说这次期末考试没有标准答案，他让我们写一篇文章，谈谈自己对二十一世纪汉语教学的看法。我用上了在教育公司的兼职经验，写了很多与汉语云教育有关的内容，正好向张教授请教请教。

考完试，我们终于放寒假了，我计划好好放松一下。晚上黄丽带我去看了一场音乐舞蹈表演，说这是他们最后一天在上海演出了。由于观众特别多，我们买票又买得比较晚，所以已经没有好座位了。不过，即使我们坐在最后排，演员们的舞蹈动作还是看得很清楚。男演员们都很有力气，甚至把女演员们举起来了好几次。演员们表演得精彩极了！

看演出的时候，我收到了欧文的信息。他说上个月他骑车摔伤了，幸亏没什么严重的问题，现在已经完全好了。我打算寒假去北京找他，这样正好可以跟他一起过春节！读硕士的时候，我们一起在上海过了三次春节。听说北方的春节跟南方的很不一样，我想去看看！

词汇 3 Vocabulary 3

1	舞蹈	wǔdǎo	*n.*	dance (HSK6 Word)
2	表演	biǎoyǎn	*n.*	performance; acting
			v.	to act; to perform; to play

3	演出	yǎnchū	*v.*	to perform
			n.	performance
4	观众	guānzhòng	*n.*	audience
5	座位	zuòwei	*n.*	seat
6	演员	yǎnyuán	*n.*	actor or actress
7	力气	lìqi	*n.*	(physical) strength; force
8	甚至	shènzhì	*conj.*	even
9	举	jǔ	*v.*	to raise up; to lift up
10	精彩	jīngcǎi	*adj.*	brilliant

语 法 Grammar

补语结构小结（Summary of Complements）

汉语里的补语结构主要有结果补语（表示动作变化产生的结果）、状态补语（动作使主语出现的情态）、趋向补语（动作行为的方向）、可能补语（可能或不可能完成）、程度补语（动作的程度）、时量补语（动作发生的时长）和动量补语（动作发生的次数）等。例如：

The complement structure in Chinese mainly includes result complement (representing the result of action or change), state complement (the modality that the action causes the subject to appear), directional complement (direction of action), possibility complement (possible or impossible to complete), degree complement (the degree of the action), duration complement (the length of time the action occurs), and the frequency complement (the number of times the action occurs), etc. For example,

1. 我昨晚复习得太晚了，刚才还在做梦呢。
2. 考完了咱们下午去逛街吧？
3. 我们一起在上海过了三次春节。

走近中国 A Touch of China

中国高考

中国的普通高等学校招生全国统一考试，简称“高考”，考试时间一般为每年 6 月 7 日至 8 日，是合格的高中毕业生或具有同等学力的考生参加的选拔性考试。当前在中国大部分省市区通行的高考方案为“3+X”。“3”指“语文、数学、外语”，“X”指由学生根据自己的意愿，自主从文科综合（分为思想政治、历史、地理）和理科综合（分为物理、化学、生物）中选择一个作为考试科目。该方案是到 2019 年止中国应用最广、最成熟的高考方案，总分 750 分（其中语文 150 分，数学 150 分，外语 150 分，文科综合 / 理科综合 300 分）。高考得分是学生进入中国普通高等学校的主要依据。各个大学会设定各自的录取分数线，考生可根据自己的考分选报相应的学校。由于高考分数将决定考生最终被哪所大学录取，因此高考在中国被形容为“千军万马过独木桥”，受到学生和家长的高度重视，并对中国的基础教育产生了极其深远的影响。

中国现代高考制度的建立有两个重要来源：一是历史上科举考试制度形成的传统考试思维和价值观，二是西方现代考试制度的模式和手段。中国有 1300 多年科举考试的历史，用于选拔人才。1905 年，出于发展新教育、培养实用人才的需要，科举制度被废除，西方的考试制度随之被引进和推广。知识改变命运，实现社会流动，促进社会公平，是高考的要义。高考在实现中国的社会公平和教育公平中发挥了重要作用，高考使数以亿计的考生通过自己的努力走出了大山，实现了上大学和看世界的梦想。

多年来，高考的形式也在不断改进。目前，中国高考仍有应试教育的弊端，文理分科也不断被社会诟病，各种改革方案还在积极探讨的过程中。相信随着中国教育现代化的发展，中国各地的高考制度也会越来越完善。

The National College Entrance Examination in China

The shorter name of the National College Entrance Examination (NCEE) in China is "Gao Kao", which usually takes place on June 7th to 8th each year. It is a selective examination for qualified high school graduates or candidates with the same academic ability. The current NCEE scheme in most provinces and municipalities in China is "3+X". "3" refers to Chinese, Mathematics and Foreign Languages, and "X" refers to the Art Comprehensive (divided into Politics, History and Geography) and Science Comprehensive (divided into Physics, Chemistry and Biology). This program is the most widely-used and most mature program in China by 2019. The total score is 750 points (150 points for Chinese, 150 points for Mathematics, 150 points for Foreign Languages, and 300 points for Art/Science Comprehensive). The NCEE score is the main basis to select students to enter China's ordinary colleges and universities. Each university will set its own admission score line, and candidates can apply to them according to their own test scores. As the scores will determine which university the candidate will ultimately be admitted to, NCEE is described as "thousands of people crossing a single-plank bridge". It is highly valued by students and parents and has a profound impact on China's basic education.

There are two important sources for the establishment of NCEE system: one is the traditional examination thinking and value formed by the Imperial Examination system in history, and the other is the mode and means of the western style modern examination system. China has more than 1300 years of Imperial Examination history, which are used to select talents. In 1905, due to the need to develop new education and cultivate practical talents, the Imperial Examination system was abolished, and the western style examination system was introduced and promoted. Knowledge can change one's fate, enhance social mobility, and promote social fairness, which is exactly the essence of NCEE. It has played an important role in realizing China's social equity and educational equity, by enabling millions of candidates to walk out of poverty through their own efforts and realize their dreams of going to university and seeing the bigger world.

Over the years, the form of NCEE has also been continuously improved.

At present, it still has the drawbacks of test-oriented education, the divided arts and sciences paths are constantly being criticized. However, various reform plans are being actively discussed. It is believed that with the development of China's education modernization, the NCEE system will be improved significantly across China.

注 释 Notes

Kējǔ zhìdù
科举 制度

The Imperial Examination System

科举制度是古代中国通过考试选拔官吏的制度，于1905年废除，影响至日本和越南等国家。科举制度是封建时代采取的最公平的人才选拔形式，扩展了国家选拔人才的社会层面，吸收了大量出身中下层社会的人才。

The Imperial Examination system was a system used in ancient China to select officials through examinations. It was abolished in 1905 and affected other countries such as Japan and Vietnam. The Imperial Examination system is the fairest form of talent selection that adopted in the feudal era. It has expanded the social dimension of the country's selection of talents and has absorbed a large number of talents from the middle and lower classes.

学而时习之 Practice Makes Progress

(一) 选词填空 (Choose the correct words for the blanks)

A. 敲　　B. 精彩　　C. 座位　　D. 梦

1. 演员们表演得非常(　　)。
2. 我们买票买得晚，已经没好(　　)了。
3. 我刚才还在做(　　)，不想起床。
4. 好像有人在(　　)门，你去看看。

（二）连词成句（Form sentences with the words given）

1. 表演　了　看　我们　场　一

______

2. 她　好了　弄　已经　牙膏　把

______

3. 他　文章　交　一篇　让　学生

______

4. 仔细　考试　看　的时候　题目　要

______

（三）阅读理解（Read and choose the right option）

安娜在上海读博士已经一个学期了，最近参加了期末考试。张教授让大家写一篇文章讨论汉语教学。安娜用上了在教育公司的兼职经历。考完试，安娜跟同学去看了一场精彩的音乐舞蹈表演。

1. 根据上文，期末考试是什么？（　　）

A. 演讲　B. 表演　C. 写文章　D. 读文章

2. 音乐舞蹈表演怎么样？（　　）

A. 精彩　B. 难看　C. 无聊　D. 紧张

（四）口语练习（Speaking task）

请用下面的词，向你的小组介绍一次汉语考试，并选择两个句子写下来。

A. 填空　B. 判断
C. 知识　D. 答案

1. ______

2. ______

（五）看图写句子（Look at the pictures and make sentences with the words given）

响

____

梦

____

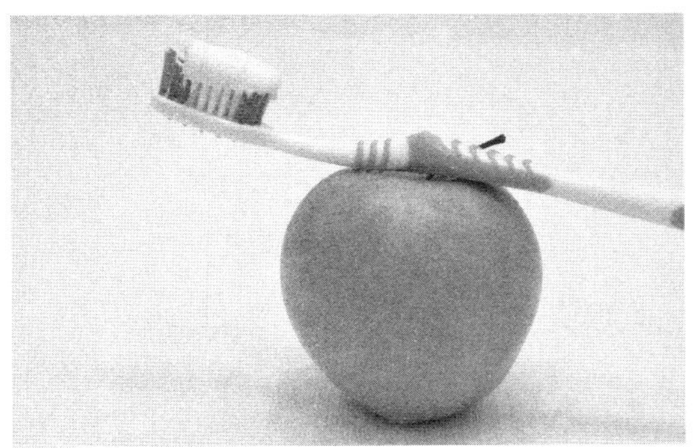

牙膏

____

演出

____

第十一课　把“福”字倒过来贴在窗户上

学习目标 Learning Objectives

1. 掌握庆祝春节相关词汇

Understand the vocabulary related to celebrating Spring Festival

2. 正确运用各种“把”字句表示对特定事物的影响或处置

Use various *Ba*-sentences to indicate the agent’s influence on certain objects correctly and appropriately

Text 1

跟欧文视频聊天

安娜：欧文，好久没跟你视频聊天了，你的胳膊好了吗？

欧文：你看，完全好了，不用担心！你放寒假了吧？

安娜：是的，刚考完期末考试。张教授让大家写一篇文章，我把兼职经验都写进去了，结果拿了满分！

欧文：你太厉害了！听说张教授很严格，每次考试只给一个学生满分。

安娜：我本来只是抱着试一试的态度写我对汉语云教育的看法，没想到张教授竟然把这个满分给我了！同学们都很吃惊。

欧文：不过你别得意，也许因为你是外国人，张教授把满分的标准降低了。

安娜：是的，但我还是很开心！这至少说明我是一名合格的博士生。

欧文：祝贺你，安娜！春节你打算怎么过？

安娜：去年是李明把一切都安排好了，但是今年我不想麻烦他。

欧文：正好我的房东说他们的儿子无法回国过春节，让我跟他们一起过。你来北京跟我们一起庆祝春节吧！

安娜：合适吗？那我住在哪里呢？

欧文：我会提前跟房东打好招呼，租几天他的客房。要是他不反对，明天我就把那个小房间收拾出来。

安娜：太棒了！那暂时这么定了，你的房东一同意，我马上就买票。

欧文：别买高铁票，最好买机票。我的房东家离机场比较近。

安娜：可我真的很讨厌坐飞机，尤其是飞机降落的时候我特别受不了。

欧文：好吧，那你坐高铁过来，到时候我去高铁站接你。

安娜：好的，谢谢你！

词汇 1　Vocabulary 1

1	视频	shìpín	*n.*	video (HSK6 Word)
2	抱	bào	*v.*	to hug; to embrace
3	得意	déyì	*adj.*	complacent
4	合格	hégé	*adj.*	qualified; up to standard
5	庆祝	qìngzhù	*v.*	to celebrate (HSK5 Word)
6	打招呼	dǎ zhāohu		to greet someone; to give prior notice
7	暂时	zànshí	*adj.*	temporary
8	高铁 *	gāotiě	*n.*	high speed rail
9	讨厌	tǎoyàn	*v.*	to dislike
10	受不了	shòubuliǎo	*v.*	to be unable to bear; can't stand

课文 2 Text 2

在北京高铁站

安娜：欧文，我下高铁了，你在哪里？

欧文：我在加油站给车加油，你出来以后往高铁站入口方向走，那边有一个天桥，你在天桥下面等我一下，我马上到。

安娜：好的。

欧文：哈哈哈，安娜！你怎么一直抱着行李箱走啊？怎么不拉着呢？

安娜：别笑话我了。刚才下车的时候，我一不小心把行李箱撞破了，没办法只好抱着走，重死了！

欧文：快给我吧，我把它放进车里。

安娜：好的，谢谢！这是你的车吗？

欧文：不是，是我的房东王教授的车。他说他家离高铁站太远了，一定要把车借给我，让我开车来接你。

安娜：太感谢王教授了。

欧文：我们现在顺便去超市买一些春节用的"福"字，明天需要用。

安娜：好的！

词汇 2 Vocabulary 2

1	加油站	jiāyóuzhàn	*n.*	gas station
2	入口	rùkǒu	*n.*	entrance; entry
3	方向	fāngxiàng	*n.*	direction
4	桥	qiáo	*n.*	bridge
5	拉	lā	*v.*	to pull
6	笑话	xiàohua	*v.*	to laugh at; to mock
			n.	joke

7	破	pò	*v.*	to break
			adj.	broken; damaged
8	死	sǐ	*v.*	to die; to be dead
			adj.	dead; used as a degree complement to show extremity

课文 3 Text 3

在北京庆祝春节

上个周末，我来到北京，准备跟欧文一起在他的房东王教授家庆祝春节。王教授和张阿姨特别热情地跟我打招呼，不仅把客房空出来允许我免费住，还把车借给欧文让他带我在北京到处逛逛。我特别感动！

昨天，我和欧文帮着房东一起收拾客厅，打扫房间，还把饼干、巧克力都装进红色的袋子里。张阿姨把窗户擦得十分干净，她让我们把“福”字贴到窗户上。我和欧文各贴了一个“福”字，觉得漂亮极了。结果，张阿姨却笑了，说我们把“福”字的方向贴错了。

原来，中国人故意把“福”字倒过来贴在窗户或门上，以表示“福到”之意。由于“福”和“富”读起来差不多，“倒”和“到”读起来也差不多，“福倒”了就表示“福到”了、“富到”了。张阿姨还提到，春节的时候，中国人的饭桌上会摆上鱼但故意剩下不吃完，这是“年年有余”的意思。她还专门给我和欧文准备了红包。她告诉我，现在中国人的生活条件好了，很多年轻人喜欢在外面吃饭庆祝春节，都不太重视怎么贴“福”字了。

我觉得倒贴“福”字是中国文化中很重要的一部分，我以前竟然没有注意到。我之前只知道中国人喜欢幸运数字，没想到还有这么多有趣的事，看来我要学习的东西还有很多！

词汇 3 Vocabulary 3

1	允许	yǔnxǔ	*v.*	to allow
2	饼干	bǐnggān	*n.*	cookies; crackers
3	巧克力	qiǎokèlì	*n.*	chocolate
4	贴 *	tiē	*v.*	to paste; to post
5	以	yǐ	*prep.*	via; by means of
			conj.	in order to; used for
6	摆	bǎi	*v.*	to arrange; to exhibit (HSK5 Word)
7	条件	tiáojiàn	*n.*	condition
8	部分	bùfen	*n.*	part; portion
9	数字	shùzì	*n.*	number

语法 Grammar

"把"字句小结（S + *Ba* + O + Verb + Additional Information）

"把"字句是汉语中的一种特殊句型，常用来强调施事者对受事者的动作造成了状态上的影响或位置上的移动等。"把"字句中的受事一般是已知或特定的，后面可以加结果补语、趋向补语等补充信息。例如：

The *Ba*-sentence is often used to describe what happened to the object in some detail. The object of *Ba*-sentence should be known or mentioned previously. Result complements and direction complements can be added to provide more detailed information. For example,

1. 安娜把兼职经验写进文章里了。
2. 安娜和欧文把贴"福"字的方向弄错了。
3. 张阿姨让他们把"福"字倒过来贴在窗户上。

走近中国　A Touch of China

汉语谐音文化

谐音作为一种语言现象，普遍存在于各种语言之中，而唯有汉语将谐音发挥得淋漓尽致。汉语中存在丰富的音同或音近字（词），深受农耕文化和儒家思想影响的汉民族有着语言崇拜、委婉含蓄、趋利避害、祈福求吉的民族心理，这些都为谐音的理解和接受创造了条件。

汉语谐音现象涉及社会文化生活的诸多方面。第一，在言语表达技巧方面，谐音使口头语言灵动起来，在某种程度上抵消了原词的负面效应，丰富了汉民族语言的趣味性，使得人们的交流更具有人情味。例如普通话中的“杯具”是指“装水的器具”，与“悲剧”一词相谐，但其蕴含的不如意、不顺心等含义就淡化多了。又如“桑心（伤心）”也属此列。“驴友（旅友）”则形象地刻画了年轻的旅游爱好者们不畏艰辛、自得其乐的形象，令人忍俊不禁。第二，在文学艺术方面，诗词歌赋、戏剧小说、楹联谜语、相声小品，都与谐音有着不解之缘。比如，刘禹锡在《竹枝词》中写道：“道是无晴却有晴”，“晴”与“情”同音，表面上是写杨柳青青、江平如镜的清丽景色，实际上含蓄地表达了女子对待爱人那种羞而不露的内在感情。第三，在日常生活方面，一些汉语字（词）通过谐音而具有吉祥的含义，满足了汉民族祈福求吉的心理。如：数字“八”谐音“发”，凡是有华人的地方都视“八”为吉祥数字，有兴旺发达的寓意，成为各种号码中的宠儿。汉族人结婚时，通常把枣子、花生、桂圆、莲子放在新床的被子上，以得到“早（枣）生贵（桂）子”的含义，表达了亲人与友人希望这对新人早日开枝散叶的美好祝愿。

总之，谐音存在坚实的文化基础，它在多领域的拓展一定意义上可以说已内化为中华文化的内在要素。没有谐音的参与，中国人的生活将失色不少。

Chinese Homophonic Culture

Homophony is a linguistic phenomenon that exists in various languages, and only Chinese can make the most of homophony. There are a wealth of characters and words with the same or similar sounds in Chinese. The Han nationality, which is deeply influenced by agricultural culture and Confucianism, has a national psychology of language worship, euphemism and implicitness, seeking advantages and avoiding disadvantages, and praying for good fortune. These have created conditions for the understanding and acceptance of homophony.

The phenomenon of Chinese homophony involves many aspects of social and cultural life. First, in terms of verbal expression skills, homophony makes the spoken language agile, offsets the negative effects of the original words to a certain extent, enriches the interest of the Chinese national language, and makes people's communication more humane. For example, the Mandarin word "cups" refers to "tool for holding water", which has the same pronunciation with the word "tragedy", but the unsatisfactory meaning is much lessened. Another example is "sad". "Travel Friends" vividly portrays young travel enthusiasts who are not afraid of hardships and enjoy themselves, which is quite amusing. Second, in terms of literature and art, poetry, drama, novels, couplet riddles, cross talk sketches, all have an indissoluble bond with homophony. For example, Liu Yuxi wrote in the poem "Zhu Zhi Ci" (Bamboo Branch Song): "They say it's raining, but I say the sun never shines in vain!" Through the homophony of "sunny" and "sentiment", the surface is the clear and beautiful scenery. In fact, it expresses the inner shy feelings of a woman who thinks of her lover. Third, in daily life, some Chinese characters and words have auspicious meanings through homophonic sounds, which suits the Han nationality's mentality of praying for good fortune. For example, the number "eight" is homophonic "fa". Wherever there are Chinese people, "eight" is regarded as a lucky number, which has the meaning of prosperity and has become the darling of various numbers. When Han people get married, they usually put dates, peanuts, longan and lotus seeds on the quilt of the new bed to get the meaning of "giving birth to babies early", which expresses the hope of relatives and friends that the couple will bring offspring to the bigger family soon.

In short, homophony has a solid cultural foundation. It can be said that it has been internalized as an inherent element of Chinese culture in a certain sense of its expansion in multiple fields. Without the influence of homophony, the life of the Chinese people will be less interesting.

Notes

Niánnián-yǒuyú
年年 有余

Abundance Every Year

“年年有余”是一个成语，表示生活富足，每年都有多余的粮食和财富，是中国传统吉祥祈福最具代表的语言之一。鱼，之所以为中国人所喜爱，除了它的食用价值外，还由于它是一种美好的文化象征。中国人的年画中常有莲花和鱼的图案，代表“莲莲有鱼”（即年年有余）。

“年年有余” is an idiom that expresses abundance in life and can be used to pray for extra food and wealth every year. It is one of the most representative languages of traditional Chinese auspicious blessings. Fish is favored by Chinese people. In addition to its edible value, it is a beautiful cultural symbol. Chinese New Year paintings often have lotus and fish patterns, which represents “Fish in lotus” (i.e. there is abundance every year).

学而时习之 Practice Makes Progress

（一）选词填空（Choose the correct words for the blanks）

A. 庆祝　　B. 笑话　　C. 暂时　　D. 倒

1. “福”字应该（　　）过来贴。
2. 我（　　）不想出国留学，以后有机会再去。
3. 欧文让安娜去北京跟他一起（　　）春节。
4. 他说的（　　）很有意思，我们都笑了。

（二）连词成句（Form sentences with the words given）

1.“福”字　倒过来　把　贴　应该

____

2. 他　打招呼　热情地　跟我

____

3. 我们　饼干　把　袋子里　装进

____

4. 不小心　安娜　箱子　坏了　撞　把

____

（三）阅读理解（Read and choose the right option）

欧文让安娜去北京跟他一起庆祝春节。房东王教授和张阿姨特别热情，把车借给欧文去接安娜。他们买了“福”字回家。张阿姨说中国人故意把“福”字倒过来贴，以求“福到”之意。安娜觉得中国文化很有意思。

1. 根据上文，“福”字应该怎么贴？（　　）

A. 正着贴　B. 倒过来贴　C. 歪着贴　D. 不用贴

2. 安娜觉得中国文化怎么样？（　　）

A. 很好　B. 很难　C. 很有趣　D. 很没意思

（四）口语练习（Speaking task）

请用下面的词，向你的小组介绍中国春节，并选择两个句子写下来。

A. 贴　B. 福
C. 红包　D. 摆

1. ______________________________

2. ______________________________

（五）看图写句子（Look at the pictures and make sentences with the words given）

合格

____

允许

____

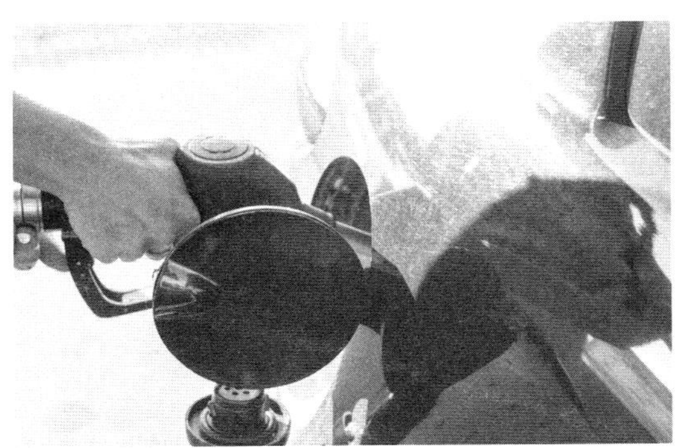

加油站

____

巧克力

____

第十二课　生活中已经出现了爱情

学习目标 Learning Objectives

1. 掌握做生意与竞争相关词汇

Understand the vocabulary related to doing business and competition

2. 正确运用各种存现句型表示人或事物的存在、出现与消失

Use various existential structures to indicate the existence, appearance and disappearance of people or things correctly and appropriately

课文 1 Text 1

在王教授书房里

欧文：安娜，你看，这是王教授的书房，这里有许多与科学研究有关的书。地上还摆着许多植物。

安娜：这是张阿姨年轻时候的照片吗？真漂亮！他们是怎么认识的？

欧文：他们是在医院通过别人介绍认识的。

安娜：真的假的？

欧文：我没骗你。三十多年前，王教授的爷爷生病住院了，张阿姨正好是那儿的护士。她把王爷爷照顾得特别好，王爷爷很喜欢她，就把她介绍给自己的孙子了。

安娜：然后她就和王教授在一起了吗？

欧文：是啊，王教授当时大学刚毕业，他说张阿姨就是他理想中的女朋

友，几年后他们就结婚了。

安娜：也就是说，张阿姨和自己照顾的病人成了亲戚。这个过程真浪漫！他们有几个孩子？

欧文：只有一个。他们本来想要个女儿，但到孩子出生才知道性别，原来是个儿子。

安娜：就是在国外留学的那个儿子对吧？

欧文：对，现在我住的那间就是他以前的房间。

安娜：那你千万别像读硕士的时候那么懒！一定要把他的房间收拾得干干净净的。

欧文：你别笑话我了！我现在每天都花一个小时打扫房间，顺便减肥。

安娜：你看起来确实瘦了不少！

词汇 1 Vocabulary 1

1	科学	kēxué	*n.*	science
			adj.	scientific; rational
2	骗	piàn	*v.*	to cheat; to deceive
3	孙子	sūnzi	*n.*	grandson
4	理想	lǐxiǎng	*n.*	dream
			adj.	ideal; desirable
5	亲戚	qīnqi	*n.*	relatives
6	过程	guòchéng	*n.*	process
7	出生	chūshēng	*v.*	to be born
8	性别	xìngbié	*n.*	gender
9	懒	lǎn	*adj.*	lazy
10	减肥	jiǎnféi	*v.*	to lose weight

课文 2 Text 2

李明开公司了

李明：喂，安娜，好久不见。你最近怎么样？

安娜：挺好的。我来北京跟欧文一起过春节了。听他说你换工作了？

李明：嗯，之前的那个工作收入不太理想，而且我与同事之间发生了一些矛盾。

安娜：啊？我记得你脾气特别好，怎么会和同事有矛盾呢？

李明：等你回上海了，咱们见面再细聊。后来我就跟一个亲戚一起开了个小公司。做生意一直是我的理想。

安娜：很好，我支持你追求自己的理想。你的公司是做什么的？

李明：主要是做一些小商品生意。

安娜：自己开公司压力很大吧？

李明：是的，会有一些由竞争引起的压力，但同时也有了更多机会。

安娜：确实，现在这个社会到处都是竞争。上次在教育公司面试的时候，有六个人同时竞争一个兼职。

李明：你拿到了这个兼职，证明你是最有竞争力的那一个！

安娜：那还要感谢你帮我介绍这个面试机会。下次我请你吃饭。

李明：等你哪天有空，咱们一起去海洋公园玩儿吧！正好我拿一些小商品出来，请你帮我看看外国人究竟喜欢哪些。

安娜：好的，没问题！

词汇 2 Vocabulary 2

1	收入	shōurù	*n.*	income; earning

2	矛盾	máodùn	*n.*	conflict; contradiction
			adj.	contradictory (HSK5 Word)
3	脾气	píqi	*n.*	temper
4	生意	shēngyi	*n.*	business; trade
5	追求	zhuīqiú	*v.*	to pursue (HSK5 Word)
6	商品	shāngpǐn	*n.*	commodity; goods (HSK5 Word)
7	竞争	jìngzhēng	*v.*	to compete
			n.	competition
8	社会	shèhuì	*n.*	society
9	海洋	hǎiyáng	*n.*	ocean

课文 3 Text 3

去海洋公园见李明

在北京过完春节后，我就回了上海。在高铁上，我回忆着王教授与张阿姨认识的过程，觉得他们的爱情有趣而浪漫。

寒假的最后一周，李明约我去海洋公园玩。他不久前开了个小公司，专门卖小商品给外国人。他公司的小商品种类丰富，但他不确定外国人究竟喜欢哪些，因此他带了许多过来让我帮忙判断。正好海洋公园里也有许多外国游客，我们也找他们问了问建议。

然后，他跟我详细说了跟之前公司同事有矛盾的事情。原来有个老同事一直对他有意见，总是想跟他比输赢。但结果每次公司有任务，都是李明做得更好，因此那个同事就越来越讨厌李明。实际上，那个同事也挺可怜的，在公司干了很久，但能力不行，收入也一直很低，很值得同情。然而，李明不想在这些矛盾上浪费时间，就直接离开公司了。

看起来李明好像输了，但其实他赢了，因为他终于可以去追求自己的理想了。在这方面，我与李明是一样的，我来中国也是为了追求研究汉语这个梦。我觉得能坚持追求自己的理想非常值得尊重。

最后，李明把我送回学校，还留了一封手写的信给我。他表示自己想说的话都写在信里了，我看到信封上写着“我喜欢你，请相信我”。李明在信里说，他喜欢我很久了，不仅喜欢我的优点，也接受我所有的缺点。

我之前心里很矛盾，现在仔细回忆这三年，李明虽然不是特别浪漫，但脾气很好。他一直陪在我身边，丰富了我在中国的生活。无论我什么时候需要帮助，他都会马上出现。我心里知道，我对他也是有感情的。生活中出现了爱情，就应该去追求。我决定明天就去邮局给李明回一封手写的信。

词汇 3 Vocabulary 3

1	种类	zhǒnglèi	*n.*	kind; type; sort (HSK5 Word)
2	丰富	fēngfù	*v.*	to enrich
			adj.	rich; plentiful
3	输	shū	*v.*	to lose
4	赢	yíng	*v.*	to win
5	可怜	kělián	*adj.*	pitiful; pitiable
			v.	to feel sympathy
6	同情	tóngqíng	*v.*	to show sympathy
			n.	sympahy
7	信封	xìnfēng	*n.*	envelope 信：letter 封：measure word for letters
8	邮局	yóujú	*n.*	post office

语 法 Grammar

存现句小结（Summary of Existential Sentences）

汉语中的存现句常表示人或者事物的存在、出现或者消失。存现句常用句型为：处所＋有＋名词；名词＋在＋处所；处所＋动词＋着＋名词；处所＋动词＋来 / 去＋名词等。例如：

Words like "在, 有, 着, 来, 出现" can be used to describe the existence, appearance or disappearance of people or things in Mandarin. The frequently-used structures are: Place +有+ Noun; Noun + 在 + Place; Place + Verb + 着 + Noun; Place + Verb + 来 / 去 + Noun etc. For example,

1. 海洋公园里有许多外国游客。
2. 王教授书房的地上摆着许多植物。
3. 安娜觉得她的生活中已经出现了爱情。

走近中国 A Touch of China

徽商精神

徽商是中国历史上十大商帮之一，曾在中国商界舞台上盛极一时。它的成功归因于徽商精神。徽商精神的内核是儒家伦理道德，其中包括如下几个主要方面：

第一，开拓进取的创业精神。徽州特殊的地理环境造就了徽民坚毅顽强的品格，徽商的创业历程可形象地称之为"徽骆驼"精神，具有不畏艰难、百折不挠的特点，哪里存在商机，徽商就走向哪里。

第二，以义取利的诚信品格。徽商信誉卓著，在经商活动中表现出信实等价的交换观、诚恳谦和的交际观、一诺千金的承诺观、物美价廉的质量观和依法经营的法制观。胡雪岩将假虎骨付之一炬，胡开文徽墨厂将质量有瑕疵的徽墨沉入水池等，都体现着徽商"质量就是生命"的诚信品格。

第三，团结协作的和谐思想。徽商基本上是一个以血缘、地缘、人缘为纽带，建立起广泛而有效经商网络的商帮，形成了“团结合作、同舟共济、以众帮众、相互提携”的协作精神，具有强大的凝聚力、向心力，从而大大提高了市场竞争力。

第四，回报社会的感恩情怀。徽商热心从事社会公益事业，体现出乐善好施的美德。在家乡和侨寓地，徽商对兴办义学、筑桥修路、救灾济荒等公益事业都倾注了巨大的热情。他们经商一方，造福一片，这种行为促进了徽商与社会的良性互动，不仅提高了徽商的知名度，也为其商业发展打下了坚实的基础、拓展了更大的空间。

在市场经济蓬勃发展的今天，需要企业建立内在的道德品质标准，培养自身的精神品格。徽商精神体现出的儒商经济伦理精神，因其丰富的内涵、强大的生命力和时代价值，不仅被今天的创新创业者所推崇，更为当今中国的诸多知名企业所传承并发扬，比如义乌小商品市场的“无所不包”、电商经济领头羊阿里巴巴的“客户第一”、民族企业华为的“5G 技术创新”等，从而助力中国制造“走出去”、走向世界。

Hui Merchants Spirit

Hui Merchants is one of the top ten business groups in Chinese history, and it once flourished on the stage of the Chinese business community. Its success is attributed to the Hui Merchants spirit. The core of this spirit is Confucian ethics, which includes the following main aspects:

First, the pioneering and enterprising spirit of entrepreneurship. The special geographical environment of Huizhou has created the perseverance and tenacious character of Hui people. The entrepreneurial process of Hui Merchants can be vividly called the “Hui camel” spirit. It has the characteristics of not fearing hardships and perseverance. Where there are business opportunities, Hui Merchants will move towards there.

Second, the integrity of the moral character. Hui Merchants have an outstanding reputation. In their business activities, they exhibited a faithful and equivalent exchange view, a sincere and modest view of communication, fulfilling promises, a view of quality at low prices, and a legal view of operating in accordance with the law. Hu Xueyan burned the fake tiger bones, and Hu Kaiwen

Hui Ink Factory submerged defective inks in a pool, etc., which all embodied the honest character of Hui Merchants that “quality is vital”.

Third, the idea of unity and cooperation and harmony. Hui Merchants is basically a business group that has established a wide and effective business network with blood, geographic and personal connections as the link. It has formed a cooperative spirit of “being united and cooperative, helping each other, and supporting each other in difficult times”, which has a powerful cohesive and centripetal force. This greatly improved their market competitiveness.

Fourth, gratitude and giving back to the society. Hui Merchants are enthusiastic about social welfare undertakings, which demonstrates the virtue of benevolence and charity. In their hometowns and places where the overseas Chinese lived, Hui Merchants devoted great enthusiasm to public welfare undertakings such as building volunteer schools, building bridges and repairing roads, and disaster relief. This behavior promotes the benign interaction between Hui Merchants and the bigger society, which not only increases the reputation of merchants in Huizhou, but also lays a solid foundation for their business development and expansion.

With the vigorous development of the market economy today, companies need to establish internal moral quality standards and cultivate their own spiritual character. Because of its rich connotation, strong vitality and timeless value, the Confucian business ethics spirit embodied by the Hui Merchants spirit is not only praised by today’s innovative entrepreneurs, but also inherited and carried forward by many well-known companies in China, including the inclusive Yiwu Small Commodity Market, the “customer first” E-commerce leader Alibaba, China’s “5G technological innovator” Huawei, etc. Also, Hui Merchants spirit has helped Chinese manufacturing to go global.

学而时习之　Practice Makes Progress

（一）选词填空（Choose the correct words for the blanks）

A. 矛盾　　B. 丰富　　C. 收入　　D. 理想

1. 在中国研究汉语是安娜的（　　）。
2. 李明的上一份工作（　　）不是很理想。

3. 李明公司的小商品种类很(　　　)。

4. 李明跟他的同事关系不好，有点儿(　　　)。

(二) 连词成句 (Form sentences with the words given)

1. 做　　理想　　生意　　的　　是　　李明

____

2. 许多　　植物　　书房　　摆着　　地上

____

3. 尊重　　值得　　追求　　理想　　非常

____

4. 已经　　爱情　　出现了　　安娜的　　生活中

____

(三) 阅读理解 (Read and choose the right option)

李明跟公司的同事有矛盾，自己开了一个小商品公司。做生意是他的理想。他约安娜去海洋公园玩，请她帮忙看看外国人究竟喜欢什么样的小商品。他给了安娜一封手写的信，告诉安娜他喜欢她很久了。

1. 根据上文，李明的理想是什么？(　　)

A. 做生意　　B. 读博士　　C. 当老师　　D. 做翻译

2. 李明给了安娜什么？(　　)

A. 小商品　　B. 一封信　　C. 公司　　D. 海洋公园

(四) 口语练习 (Speaking task)

请用下面的词，向你的小组介绍一次你去公园的经历，并选择两个句子写下来。

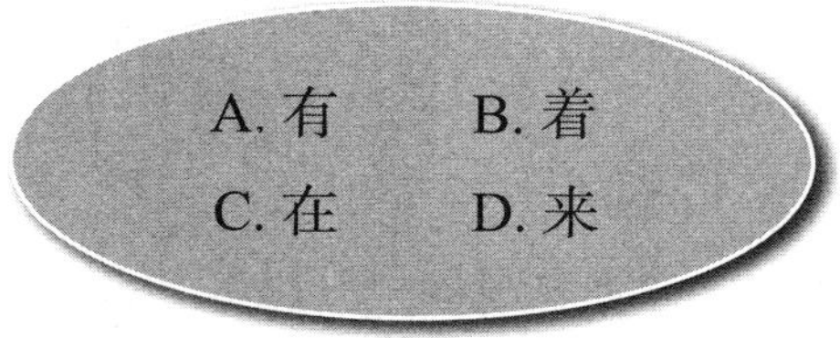

1. ____________________

2. ____________________

（五）看图写句子（Look at the pictures and make sentences with the words given）

科学

____

生意

____

赢

____

信封

____

词汇总表

生词	拼音	词类	释义	课文
A				
爱情	àiqíng	*n.*	love	L5.3
B				
百分之	bǎi fēn zhī		percent	L2.2
摆	bǎi	*v.*	to arrange; to exhibit (HSK5 Word)	L11.3
保护	bǎohù	*v.*	to protect; to safeguard	L6.1
抱	bào	*v.*	to hug; to embrace	L11.1
倍	bèi	*m.*	times; -fold	L7.3
标准	biāozhǔn	*n.*	criterion; norm	L4.3
		adj.	standard	
表格	biǎogé	*n.*	form; table	L4.2
表示	biǎoshì	*v.*	to express; to mean	L5.1
表演	biǎoyǎn	*n.*	performance; acting	L10.3
		v.	to act; to perform; to play	
表扬	biǎoyáng	*v.*	to praise	L2.3
饼干	bǐnggān	*n.*	cookies; crackers	L11.3
部分	bùfen	*n.*	part; portion	L11.3
C				
猜	cāi	*v.*	to guess	L5.1
材料	cáiliào	*n.*	material	L2.3
厕所	cèsuǒ	*n.*	toilet	L7.3

续表

生词	拼音	词类	释义	课文
场	chǎng	*m.*	measure word for sporting or recreational activities; measure word for exams, rain, snow, etc.	L9.2
		n.	large place used for a specific purpose; stage; scene (of a play)	
成为	chéngwéi	*v.*	to become	L2.2
诚实	chéngshi	*adj.*	honest	L4.3
吃惊	chījīng	*v.*	to be shocked 吃：to eat　惊：surprise	L3.3
出差	chūchāi	*v.*	to go on an official or business trip	L9.2
出生	chūshēng	*v.*	to be born	L12.1
出现	chūxiàn	*v.*	to appear	L5.2
传真	chuánzhēn	*v.*	to fax	L2.2
词语	cíyǔ	*n.*	word	L7.1
粗心	cūxīn	*adj.*	careless; thoughtless	L1.2
错误	cuòwù	*n.*	error; mistake	L7.2

D

生词	拼音	词类	释义	课文
答案	dá'àn	*n.*	answer	L10.1
打扰	dǎrǎo	*v.*	to disturb; to bother; to trouble	L9.1
打印	dǎyìn	*v.*	to print	L1.2
打招呼	dǎ zhāohu		to greet someone; to give prior notice	L11.1
戴	dài	*v.*	to wear; to put on	L8.1
倒	dào	*v.*	to throw away	L8.1
道歉	dàoqiàn	*v.*	to apologize 道：to say　歉：apology	L6.1
得意	déyì	*adj.*	complacent	L11.1
得	děi	*aux.*	ought to; need to	L1.1
登机牌	dēngjī pái		boarding pass 登机：to board　牌：card	L1.2

续表

生词	拼音	词类	释义	课文
低	dī	*adj.*	low	L3.1
		v.	to lower	
底	dǐ	*n.*	bottom; base; end (of the month, year, etc.)	L9.1
地球	dìqiú	*n.*	the Earth	L8.2
调查	diàochá	*v.*	to investigate; to survey	L7.3
		n.	investigation; survey	
掉	diào	*v.*	to drop; to lag behind	L5.2
肚子	dùzi	*n.*	stomach; belly	L8.1
对话	duìhuà	*v.*	to have a dialogue or conversation	L9.1
对面	duìmiàn	*n.*	the opposite side	L7.3
对于	duìyú	*prep.*	with regards to	L3.3

E

生词	拼音	词类	释义	课文
而	ér	*conj.*	indicating causal relation or contrast	L2.3

F

生词	拼音	词类	释义	课文
发票	fāpiào	*n.*	invoice (HSK5 Word)	L2.1
发生	fāshēng	*v.*	to happen; to take place	L4.3
烦恼	fánnǎo	*n.*	trouble	L5.2
		adj.	worried; distressed	
反对	fǎnduì	*v.*	to fight against; to oppose; to be opposed to; to disagree with	L9.1
方式	fāngshì	*n.*	way; manner; style; mode (HSK5 Word)	L9.1
方向	fāngxiàng	*n.*	direction	L11.2
房东	fángdōng	*n.*	landlord	L1.3
放弃	fàngqì	*v.*	to abandon; to give up	L3.1
分类 *	fēnlèi	*v.*	to classify	L8.2
丰富	fēngfù	*v.*	to enrich	L12.3
		adj.	rich; plentiful	

续表

生词	拼音	词类	释义	课文
父亲	fùqin	*n.*	father	L9.1
负责	fùzé	*v.*	to be in charge of	L2.3
复印	fùyìn	*v.*	to duplicate; to photocopy	L2.2
富	fù	*adj.*	rich	L8.3

G

生词	拼音	词类	释义	课文
敢	gǎn	*aux.*	dare	L5.1
感动	gǎndòng	*v.*	to make someone feel touched	L2.3
		adj.	touched	
感情	gǎnqíng	*n.*	emotion; sentiment; affection; feelings between two persons	L9.3
感谢	gǎnxiè	*v.*	to thank; to be grateful	L2.2
干	gàn	*v.*	to do one's job	L4.2
高铁 *	gāotiě	*n.*	high speed rail	L11.1
胳膊	gēbo	*n.*	arm	L6.1
各	gè	*pron.*	each; every	L8.2
工资	gōngzī	*n.*	wage; salary	L2.2
估计	gūjì	*v.*	to estimate	L6.2
鼓励	gǔlì	*v.*	to encourage	L2.3
		n.	encouragement	
故意	gùyì	*adv.*	deliberately; on purpose	L6.3
观众	guānzhòng	*n.*	audience	L10.3
管理	guǎnlǐ	*v.*	to manage	L8.2
广播	guǎngbō	*n.*	broadcast; broadcasting	L6.3
		v.	to broadcast; to be on the air	
过程	guòchéng	*n.*	process	L12.1

续表

生词	拼音	词类	释义	课文
			H	
海洋	hǎiyáng	*n.*	ocean	L12.2
合格	hégé	*adj.*	qualified; up to standard	L11.1
合同	hétong	*n.*	contract (HSK5 Word)	L2.2
护士	hùshi	*n.*	nurse	L1.3
怀疑	huáiyí	*v.*	to suspect	L7.2
回忆	huíyì	*v.*	to recall	L6.3
火	huǒ	*n.*	fire	L7.1
		adj.	popular	
获得	huòdé	*v.*	to obtain; to gain	L6.3
			J	
积极	jījí	*adj.*	active; positive	L3.1
积累	jīlěi	*v.*	to accumulate	L2.3
激动	jīdòng	*adj.*	excited; emotional	L1.1
即使	jíshǐ	*conj.*	even if; even though	L3.1
系	jì	*v.*	to tie; to fasten (HSK5 Word)	L1.1
加油站	jiāyóuzhàn	*n.*	gas station	L11.2
兼职	jiānzhí	*n.*	part-time job (HSK5 Word)	L4.2
减肥	jiǎnféi	*v.*	to lose weight	L12.1
减少	jiǎnshǎo	*v.*	to reduce; to decrease	L8.2
将来	jiānglái	*n.*	future	L6.1
奖金	jiǎngjīn	*n.*	reward; bonus	L4.2
奖学金 *	jiǎngxuéjīn	*n.*	scholarship	L4.1
降低	jiàngdī	*v.*	to reduce; to bring down	L4.3
交	jiāo	*v.*	to make friends; to hand over; to submit	L10.1
交流	jiāoliú	*v.*	to communicate; to exchange	L9.2

续表

生词	拼音	词类	释义	课文
骄傲	jiāo'ào	*adj.*	proud; conceited	L9.1
		n.	pride; a person or thing worth being proud of	
教授	jiàoshòu	*n.*	professor	L1.3
教育	jiàoyù	*v.*	to educate	L4.2
		n.	education	
节	jié	*m.*	section	L7.1
结果	jiéguǒ	*n.*	result	L3.3
		conj.	in the end	
解释	jiěshì	*v.*	to explain	L4.3
紧张	jǐnzhāng	*adj.*	nervous	L2.1
进行	jìnxíng	*v.*	to carry out; to conduct	L8.2
经验	jīngyàn	*n.*	experience	L2.2
精彩	jīngcǎi	*adj.*	brilliant	L10.3
竞争	jìngzhēng	*v.*	to compete	L12.2
		n.	competition	
究竟	jiūjìng	*adv.*	on earth	L7.1
举	jǔ	*v.*	to raise up; to lift up	L10.3
举办	jǔbàn	*v.*	to conduct; to hold	L9.2
举行	jǔxíng	*v.*	to hold (a meeting, ceremony, etc.)	L6.2
拒绝	jùjué	*v.*	to decline; to reject	L5.1

K

生词	拼音	词类	释义	课文
看法	kànfa	*n.*	perspective; view; opinion	L9.3
考虑	kǎolǜ	*v.*	to consider	L5.2
科学	kēxué	*n.*	science	L12.1
		adj.	scientific; rational	

续表

生词	拼音	词类	释义	课文
可怜	kělián	*adj.*	pitiful; pitiable	L12.3
		v.	to feel sympathy	
可惜	kěxī	*adj.*	regrettable; unfortunate	L3.1
空	kòng	*v.*	to empty	L1.3
	kòng	*n.*	free time; space	
	kōng	*adj.*	vacant; unoccupied; empty	
恐怕	kǒngpà	*v.*	to worry	L6.2
		adv.	I'm afraid that...	
苦	kǔ	*adj.*	bitter	L2.2
困	kùn	*adj.*	sleepy	L10.2
		v.	to trap; to be in trouble	
困难	kùnnan	*adj.*	difficult; hard	L3.1
		n.	difficulty; hardship	

L

生词	拼音	词类	释义	课文
拉	lā	*v.*	to pull	L11.2
来自	láizì	*v.*	to come from	L9.3
懒	lǎn	*adj.*	lazy	L12.1
浪漫	làngmàn	*adj.*	romantic	L5.3
冷静	lěngjìng	*adj.*	calm; cool-headed	L6.3
礼拜天	lǐbàitiān	*n.*	Sunday 礼拜：week 天：day	L5.2
礼貌	lǐmào	*n.*	manners; politeness	L5.1
		adj.	polite	
理解	lǐjiě	*v.*	to understand; to comprehend	L7.2
理论	lǐlùn	*n.*	theory (HSK5 Word)	L10.1

续表

生词	拼音	词类	释义	课文
理想	lǐxiǎng	*n.*	dream	L12.1
		adj.	ideal; desirable	
力气	lìqi	*n.*	(physical) strength; force	L10.3
例如	lìrú	*v.*	for example; for instance; such as	L9.2
凉快	liángkuai	*adj.*	cool	L3.2
另外	lìngwài	*pron.*	other; another	L9.3
		adv.	besides; moreover	
		conj.	furthermore; in addition	
留	liú	*v.*	to stay; to remain	L1.3
流利	liúlì	*adj.*	fluent	L2.1
流行	liúxíng	*adj.*	fashionable; popular	L3.2
		v.	to become popular; (of a contagious disease, etc.) to spread	
M				
马虎	mǎhu	*adj.*	careless; negligent	L1.3
满	mǎn	*adj.*	full; filled; packed	L9.1
		v.	to fill; to reach the limit	
		adv.	fully; completely; quite	
毛巾	máojīn	*n.*	towel	L10.2
矛盾	máodùn	*n.*	conflict; contradiction	L12.2
		adj.	contradictory (HSK5 Word)	
梦	mèng	*n.*	dream	L10.2
		v.	to dream	

续表

生词	拼音	词类	释义	课文
面试 *	miànshì	*n.*	interview	L1.1
		v.	to interview	
秒	miǎo	*m.*	second (unit of time)	L3.2
目的	mùdì	*n.*	purpose; aim	L3.2
			N	
耐心	nàixīn	*adj.*	patient	L3.2
		n.	patience	
难道	nándào	*adv.*	indicating an interrogating tone of rhetorical question	L5.1
难怪	nánguài	*adv.*	no wonder (HSK5 Word)	L8.1
难受	nánshòu	*adj.*	uncomfortable; unwell; not feeling physically relaxed; sad 难：difficult 受：to bear	L5.3
内容	nèiróng	*n.*	content; substance	L9.2
嗯	ǹg	*int.*	indicating approval, appreciation or agreement (HSK5 Word)	L3.1
宁可	nìngkě	*adv.*	would rather (HSK5 Word)	L4.3
弄	nòng	*v.*	to do; to manage (informal)	L10.2
			O	
偶尔	ǒu'ěr	*adv.*	occasionally; once in a while	L9.3
			P	
判断	pànduàn	*v.*	to judge	L10.1
陪	péi	*v.*	to accompany	L5.3
批评	pīpíng	*v.*	to criticize	L6.3
皮肤	pífū	*n.*	skin	L8.1
脾气	píqi	*n.*	temper	L12.2
篇	piān	*m.*	measure word for articles or papers	L10.1

续表

<table>
<tr><th>生词</th><th>拼音</th><th>词类</th><th>释义</th><th>课文</th></tr>
<tr><td>骗</td><td>piàn</td><td>v.</td><td>to cheat; to deceive</td><td>L12.1</td></tr>
<tr><td>平安</td><td>píng'ān</td><td>adj.</td><td>safe and sound; well; without mishap (HSK5 Word)</td><td>L9.3</td></tr>
<tr><td rowspan="2">破</td><td rowspan="2">pò</td><td>v.</td><td>to break</td><td rowspan="2">L11.2</td></tr>
<tr><td>adj.</td><td>broken; damaged</td></tr>
<tr><td>普通话</td><td>pǔtōnghuà</td><td>n.</td><td>Mandarin (common speech of the Chinese language)</td><td>L2.1</td></tr>
<tr><td colspan="5">Q</td></tr>
<tr><td>敲</td><td>qiāo</td><td>v.</td><td>to knock</td><td>L10.2</td></tr>
<tr><td>桥</td><td>qiáo</td><td>n.</td><td>bridge</td><td>L11.2</td></tr>
<tr><td>巧克力</td><td>qiǎokèlì</td><td>n.</td><td>chocolate</td><td>L11.3</td></tr>
<tr><td>亲戚</td><td>qīnqi</td><td>n.</td><td>relatives</td><td>L12.1</td></tr>
<tr><td>情况</td><td>qíngkuàng</td><td>n.</td><td>situation; state of affairs</td><td>L6.1</td></tr>
<tr><td>请教</td><td>qǐngjiào</td><td>v.</td><td>to ask for guidance (HSK6 Word)</td><td>L7.2</td></tr>
<tr><td>庆祝</td><td>qìngzhù</td><td>v.</td><td>to celebrate (HSK5 Word)</td><td>L11.1</td></tr>
<tr><td>穷</td><td>qióng</td><td>adj.</td><td>poor; poverty-stricken</td><td>L8.3</td></tr>
<tr><td>取</td><td>qǔ</td><td>v.</td><td>to get; to fetch</td><td>L1.2</td></tr>
<tr><td>全部</td><td>quánbù</td><td>n.</td><td>all; the whole; the entire
全：whole; entire　部：part</td><td>L6.2</td></tr>
<tr><td>缺点</td><td>quēdiǎn</td><td>n.</td><td>shortcoming; weakness
缺：deficiency　点：point</td><td>L5.2</td></tr>
<tr><td>缺少</td><td>quēshǎo</td><td>v.</td><td>to lack; to be short of</td><td>L7.3</td></tr>
<tr><td rowspan="2">确定</td><td rowspan="2">quèdìng</td><td>v.</td><td>to be sure</td><td rowspan="2">L5.3</td></tr>
<tr><td>adj.</td><td>definite</td></tr>
<tr><td rowspan="2">确实</td><td rowspan="2">quèshí</td><td>adj.</td><td>reliable; true</td><td rowspan="2">L6.2</td></tr>
<tr><td>adv.</td><td>indeed; truly</td></tr>
</table>

续表

生词	拼音	词类	释义	课文
			R	
然而	rán'ér	*conj.*	nevertheless; however	L4.3
任务	rènwu	*n.*	task; mission	L7.3
仍然	réngrán	*adv.*	still; yet	L3.2
入口	rùkǒu	*n.*	entrance; entry	L11.2
			S	
晒	shài	*v.*	to bask in the sunshine (HSK5 Word)	L8.1
伤心	shāngxīn	*adj.*	sad; heart-broken 伤：to injure　心：heart	L5.3
商量	shāngliang	*v.*	to talk over; to discuss	L6.2
商品	shāngpǐn	*n.*	commodity; goods (HSK5 Word)	L12.2
社会	shèhuì	*n.*	society	L12.2
申请	shēnqǐng	*v.*	to apply for	L4.1
		n.	application	
深	shēn	*adj.*	deep	L8.1
甚至	shènzhì	*conj.*	even	L10.3
生命	shēngmìng	*n.*	life	L5.2
生意	shēngyi	*n.*	business; trade	L12.2
剩	shèng	*v.*	to be left over; to remain	L10.1
失败	shībài	*v.*	to be defeated; to fail	L4.1
		adj.	unsuccessful	
失望	shīwàng	*v.*	to feel disappointed 失：to lose　望：hope	L4.1
		adj.	disappointing	
师傅	shīfu	*n.*	master; an honorific address for older men; informal way to address drivers	L2.1

续表

生词	拼音	词类	释义	课文
实际	shíjì	*adj.*	real; actual	L7.1
实践	shíjiàn	*v.*	to practise (HSK5 Word)	L10.1
		n.	practice	
使	shǐ	*v.*	to cause; to make	L2.3
世纪	shìjì	*n.*	century	L8.3
视频	shìpín	*n.*	video (HSK6 Word)	L11.1
是否	shìfǒu	*adv.*	whether; whether or not	L4.1
收入	shōurù	*n.*	income; earning	L12.2
受不了	shòubuliǎo	*v.*	to be unable to bear; can't stand	L11.1
受到	shòudào		to receive (praise, an education, punishment, etc.)	L6.2
输	shū	*v.*	to lose	L12.3
数量	shùliàng	*n.*	quantity; amount	L7.3
数字	shùzì	*n.*	number	L11.3
摔 *	shuāi	*v.*	to fall; to drop and break	L6.1
顺序	shùnxù	*n.*	sequence; order	L9.2
说明	shuōmíng	*v.*	to explain; to illustrate; to indicate; to prove	L6.3
		n.	explanation; directions; caption	
死	sǐ	*v.*	to die; to be dead	L11.2
		adj.	dead; used as a degree complement to show extremity	
孙子	sūnzi	*n.*	grandson	L12.1
所有	suǒyǒu	*adj.*	all of; every	L5.1

T

生词	拼音	词类	释义	课文
抬	tái	*v.*	to lift; to raise; (of two or more persons) to carry	L6.2
态度	tàidu	*n.*	attitude	L3.1
讨论	tǎolùn	*v.*	to discuss; to talk over	L7.2

续表

生词	拼音	词类	释义	课文
讨厌	tǎoyàn	*v.*	to dislike	L11.1
提	tí	*v.*	to mention	L4.1
提前	tíqián	*v.*	to shift to an earlier time	L1.2
提醒	tíxǐng	*v.*	to remind	L5.3
填空	tiánkòng	*v.*	to fill in the blanks	L10.1
条件	tiáojiàn	*n.*	condition	L11.3
贴 *	tiē	*v.*	to paste; to post	L11.3
通过	tōngguò	*v.*	to pass	L1.1
		prep.	through	
通知	tōngzhī	*v.*	to inform	L4.2
		n.	notice; notification	
同情	tóngqíng	*v.*	to show sympathy	L12.3
		n.	sympathy	
同时	tóngshí	*n.*	same time	L7.3
		conj.	at the same time	
推	tuī	*v.*	to push	L1.1
推迟	tuīchí	*v.*	to postpone; to delay 推：to push 迟：late	L1.2

W

生词	拼音	词类	释义	课文
温度	wēndù	*n.*	temperature	L3.1
文章	wénzhāng	*n.*	passage; article	L3.3
污染	wūrǎn	*n.*	pollution	L8.2
		v.	to pollute	
无	wú	*v.*	to lack	L5.3
无聊	wúliáo	*adj.*	bored; boring	L3.2
无论	wúlùn	*conj.*	regardless of; no matter	L4.1

续表

生词	拼音	词类	释义	课文
舞蹈	wǔdǎo	*n.*	dance (HSK6 Word)	L10.3
误会	wùhuì	*v.*	to misunderstand	L4.2
		n.	misunderstanding	
X				
吸引	xīyǐn	*v.*	to attract	L5.2
现场	xiànchǎng	*n.*	spot; site; work field; the scene (of a crime, accident, etc.) (HSK6 Word)	L9.2
相反	xiāngfǎn	*adj.*	opposite	L8.1
		conj.	on the contrary	
响	xiǎng	*v.*	to ring; to sound	L10.2
		adj.	loud	
消息	xiāoxi	*n.*	information; news	L1.1
小伙子	xiǎohuǒzi	*n.*	young man	L2.1
笑话	xiàohua	*v.*	to laugh at; to mock	L11.2
		n.	joke	
信封	xìnfēng	*n.*	envelope 信：letter　封：measure word for letters	L12.3
信心	xìnxīn	*n.*	confidence	L3.3
兴奋	xīngfèn	*adj.*	excited; exciting	L7.3
行	xíng	*adj.*	capable; competent; okay	L4.2
醒	xǐng	*v.*	to wake up	L10.2
幸福	xìngfú	*n.*	happiness; well-being 幸：good fortune; luck　福：blessings	L9.3
		adj.	happy; blessed	
幸亏	xìngkuī	*adv.*	fortunately; luckily (HSK5 Word)	L1.3
幸运	xìngyùn	*adj.*	fortunate; lucky (HSK5 Word)	L6.3
		n.	good fortune; good luck	

续表

生词	拼音	词类	释义	课文
性别	xìngbié	*n.*	gender	L12.1
许多	xǔduō	*num.*	many; a lot of; lots of	L8.3
学期	xuéqī	*n.*	term; semester	L3.2

Y

生词	拼音	词类	释义	课文
压力	yālì	*n.*	pressure; stress	L3.3
呀	yā	*int.*	used alone to express surprise	L1.2
牙膏	yágāo	*n.*	toothpaste	L10.2
亚洲	Yàzhōu	*n.*	Asia	L8.3
严格	yángé	*adj.*	strict	L3.3
		v.	to be strict with	
严重	yánzhòng	*adj.*	serious; severe	L6.1
研究	yánjiū	*n.*	research	L1.3
		v.	to research	
眼镜	yǎnjìng	*n.*	glasses; spectacles	L8.1
演出	yǎnchū	*v.*	to perform	L10.3
		n.	performance	
演员	yǎnyuán	*n.*	actor or actress	L10.3
要不	yàobù	*conj.*	or else; how about... (HSK5 Word)	L1.2
要不是 *	yàobúshì	*conj.*	if it were not for	L1.2
也许	yěxǔ	*adv.*	perhaps; maybe	L4.1
以	yǐ	*prep.*	via; by means of	L11.3
		conj.	in order to; used for	
艺术	yìshù	*n.*	art	L7.1
意见	yìjian	*n.*	opinion; idea; complaint	L9.1
因此	yīncǐ	*conj.*	therefore; so	L7.2
引起	yǐnqǐ	*v.*	to bring; to cause	L8.2

续表

生词	拼音	词类	释义	课文
赢	yíng	*v.*	to win	L12.3
永远	yǒngyuǎn	*adv.*	forever	L9.3
		n.	eternity	
优点	yōudiǎn	*n.*	merit; advantage 优：excellent　点：point	L5.2
由	yóu	*prep.*	from	L8.2
由于	yóuyú	*conj.*	because; since	L3.3
邮局	yóujú	*n.*	post office	L12.3
友好	yǒuhǎo	*adj.*	friendly 友：friend　好：good	L2.1
友谊	yǒuyì	*n.*	friendship	L2.1
有趣	yǒuqù	*adj.*	interesting	L5.3
与	yǔ	*conj.*	and (literary equivalent of 和)	L2.3
语言	yǔyán	*n.*	language	L1.3
原来	yuánlái	*adj.*	former; original	L4.2
		adv.	It turns out that…	
原谅	yuánliàng	*v.*	to excuse; to forgive; to pardon	L6.3
约会	yuēhui	*v.*	to go on a date 约：to make an appointment　会：meeting	L5.1
阅读	yuèdú	*v.*	to read	L9.2
云	yún	*n.*	cloud	L8.3
		adj.	online	
允许	yǔnxǔ	*v.*	to allow	L11.3

Z

生词	拼音	词类	释义	课文
咱们	zánmen	*pron.*	we; us	L3.2
暂时	zànshí	*adj.*	temporary	L11.1
责任	zérèn	*n.*	duty; responsibility	L6.1

续表

生词	拼音	词类	释义	课文
增加	zēngjiā	*v.*	to raise; to increase 增：to increase; to expand　加：to add	L9.3
占线	zhànxiàn	*v.*	to be busy (telephone line) 占：to occupy　线：string; line	L6.2
真实	zhēnshí	*adj.*	true; real (HSK5 Word)	L8.3
正常	zhèngcháng	*adj.*	normal	L7.2
正式	zhèngshì	*adj.*	formal	L1.1
证明	zhèngmíng	*v.*	to prove; to testify	L8.3
之	zhī	*part.*	possessive particle (literary equivalent of 的)	L2.1
支持	zhīchí	*v.*	to be in favor of; to support	L9.1
知识	zhīshi	*n.*	knowledge	L10.1
直接	zhíjiē	*adj.*	direct	L5.1
指	zhǐ	*v.*	to point at; to refer to	L7.1
指导	zhǐdǎo	*v.*	to guide; to coach (HSK5 Word)	L7.1
种类	zhǒnglèi	*n.*	kind; type; sort (HSK5 Word)	L12.3
重点	zhòngdiǎn	*n.*	focus; key point 重：heavy　点：point	L7.2
祝贺	zhùhè	*v.*	to congratulate	L1.1
专门	zhuānmén	*adv.*	specially	L4.3
撞	zhuàng	*v.*	to run into; to bump into (HSK5 Word)	L6.1
追求	zhuīqiú	*v.*	to pursue (HSK5 Word)	L12.2
准确	zhǔnquè	*adj.*	accurate	L7.2
资料	zīliào	*n.*	material; resource; data (HSK5 Word)	L6.1
仔细	zǐxì	*adj.*	careful	L10.2
自然	zìrán	*n.*	the nature world	L7.1
		adj.	natural	
		adv.	naturally; certainly	

续表

生词	拼音	词类	释义	课文
自信	zìxìn	*n.*	self-confidence	L4.1
		adj.	self-confident	
尊重	zūnzhòng	*v.*	to respect	L3.3
		adj.	respectful	
		n.	respect	
座	zuò	*m.*	measure word for buildings or mountains	L8.3
座位	zuòwei	*n.*	seat	L10.3